Baltho

The Dog Who Owned a Man

Baltho

The Dog Who Owned a Man

Thomas Ramey Watson

Barn Swallow Media

BALTHO, THE DOG WHO OWNED A MAN

 **Barn Swallow Media**
Denver, CO

Copyright © 2012 Thomas Ramey Watson
ISBN: 0-9818430-0-1 (alk. paper)
ISBN-13: 978-0-9818430-0-1 (alk. paper)
LCCN: 2012917301

ALL RIGHTS RESERVED
No part of this publication may be reproduced, stored in a retrieval system, or transmitted in any form by any means—electronic, photocopying, recording or otherwise—without prior written consent. Please do not participate in or encourage piracy of copyrighted materials in violation of the author's rights. Purchase only authorized editions.

This book was inspired by actual events. However, certain aspects have been fictionalized.

LIBRARY OF CONGRESS CATALOGING-IN-PUBLICATION DATA
Baltho, The Dog Who Owned a Man / Thomas Ramey Watson.
p.cm.
ISBN-13: 978-0-9818430-0-1 (alk. paper)
1. Dogs. 2. Afghan hounds. 3. Pets. 4. Therapy dogs.
5. Spirituality. 6. Paranormal. I. Title.

Cover design by John Morris-Reihl
Barn swallow photo by Roger Lindsay
The cat photo on the spine is of Baltho's companion, Figaro, or Figgy.

Author's Note

This is the first in what will be at least three books about my unusual experiences with extraordinary animals that have come into my life. Most have been dogs, although I have had wonderful cats as well.

This book was inspired by actual events. However, certain aspects have been fictionalized. The essence of the story, which centers on my Afghan hound Balthazar (Baltho) and me, remains intact.

As always, I want to thank a number of people who have helped me throughout the journey, especially Alan Naslund, Carolyn Plummer, Christine Landry, Jane Ellinger, and some of my family. Spirituality writer, editor, and friend, Dianne Arcangel, has been phenomenally helpful, advising me through a number of hurdles. My editor, Michael Kaye, has also proved thorough and insightful, and Kathryn Brodrick has been an invaluable copy editor. Denver attorney, Peter Lemire, has also provided essential advice. Jenny Smedley, Catharina Jarl, Tava Hanson, and other friends I've met recently have been very supportive.

No one walks alone. I am grateful for all good folks who have listened and offered help and encouragement along the way. The book is dedicated to those who have been fortunate enough to have found themselves the human companions of animals whose love is without limit and endures all things. Nothing sorts our priorities or teaches us more.

Embracing Mystery

One giant leap—and his front paws landed on my chest. As he stared into my eyes, and I gazed into his, I knew this was the Afghan hound who had been calling me telepathically for weeks. This time, I felt him physically.

I was standing just outside the Denver Afghan Rescue. "You're here," I whispered, sensing his presence. I surveyed the grounds. Dry, tiny-leaved, Chinese elms dabbed a landscape of sagebrush and sand beneath the blazing June sun. "I know it." I walked toward the twelve-foot high, chain-link fence that surrounded the compound, giving it the air of a correctional facility.

As I neared the fence, pebbles crunched underfoot. I opened the gate and walked toward a small, wood-frame house on the west side of the grounds. Dozens of dogs barked, alerting each other and their caretakers to an intruder. I could make out the individual voices of at least fifteen dogs housed there—medium-to-low-range sounds of alarm. Their collective din was excruciating.

A man looked out the window of the house. The door opened. He stepped out into the sunlight and strode my way. He stood at least six-feet-three. He sized me up from head to foot and smiled. I guessed he was Jim, the head of the Rescue—the man I'd talked with last night on the phone. "I'm Jim." He extended his hand. His grip was firm. "Mystery's a super-sized Afghan, weighing seventy-five pounds," he said. "With the build of a linebacker, you ought to be able to handle him. You're what, six-two, maybe two-twenty?"

"Not quite—one ninety-eight."

"Well, you're big enough not to get knocked down." He looked me over again. "Maybe suffer a shoulder dislocation, but only now and then."

I laughed, hoping he was making a joke.

The name the Rescue had given the Afghan hound, Mystery, felt significant. My life was one of paradoxes and mysteries too. If we come into this life with a map, mine was one of roundabouts and detours, with few straight roads anywhere. I was at the Afghan Rescue because I hadn't been able to elude the notion that an Afghan hound was telepathically calling me, begging me, to locate and rescue him. An independent, high-maintenance Afghan wasn't the dog that I'd been planning to adopt. I'd wanted one of those popular breeds—a bouncy, responsive Golden Retriever or a Labrador.

"Mystery's down at the other end," Jim said, walking me out to the pens on the east side of the property. "You said on the phone you're a psychotherapist?" He lifted the heavy padlock on the gate, stuck in a key, and released the lock. He swung open the gate.

I nodded. "I'm just about finished with my training. Until recently, I taught English and was the Episcopal chaplain for the Auraria campus." It was 1992. The glare of the sun on the cement runs and concrete doghouses inside the individual cages made me wish I'd worn sunglasses.

"Good," Jim began. "You're complicated. You should be able to understand Mystery, if anyone can." He laughed.

"I've spent my whole life trying to understand mysteries," I said. "It seems something is always trying to outfox us, threatening our best-laid plans. I'd like to see what's ahead and avert the danger before it manifests."

Jim laughed. He closed the gate behind us. "This reminds me—you've got to be careful about latches of every kind. Mystery is smart, often too smart. He can open just about any gate. A strong padlock—kept locked—is the only guarantee of confining him."

We passed into an alley that must have stretched at least a hundred yards ahead. Individual kennels formed by six-foot high chain-link fencing lined the way. Each kennel was maybe eight-feet wide and twelve-feet deep and contained a square dog house made of cement at the back. Some kennels held one or two Afghans. Some were empty.

As we walked, I spotted a frail, small-boned, white Afghan. *There's a Snow Queen in hiding*, I thought. Her body was shaking. She stared up at me with brown, soulful eyes. She looked pitiful, so needy. The rescuer in me wanted to respond.

"The dog for you is this way," Jim said, urging me on. He was several yards ahead of me by then. The place was a labyrinth. I wondered where the Minotaur was.

We took a few more steps, and a huge, dark beast bounded from a distant side-run into our path. His long, brindle hair, as I'd learned to call it during my earlier years with an Afghan, flew from his sides like magnificent wings.

"Mystery's out!" Jim shouted—as the Afghan bounded past him toward me, barking excitedly.

I had only time to mutter, "Mystery's everywhere," before he skidded, reared up, and, with his front paws, landed on my chest. Remarkably, he was so graceful that he didn't knock me over. I did, however, feel the impact of his muscle-driven mass.

Still barking—then whimpering and yapping alternately, as if he'd found his long-lost partner and friend—he nipped at my nose, my earlobes, my chin.

"Hey," I said, "I know you're ecstatic, but take it easy with the biting. It hurts."

In the bright sunshine, his thick, dark coat showed a glossy mix of walnut browns and mahoganies, highlighted by Brazilian teaks and blonds. The hair revealed a distinct red cast.

A big white star with a long tail ran the length of his chest. His dark whiskers, also showing red highlights, formed a full and bushy beard, the greatest I'd ever sighted on an Afghan. His eyebrows must have been an inch long, and his intelligent eyes, like rich cherry wood, complemented his coat.

He began to pet me with first one paw and then the other. His toes moved upon me, massaging my skin. I noticed the huge, webbed feet that his breed had evolved. Their toes became webbed so they could gain better traction in desert sands, helping them grasp unstable terrain. Their upward-curved tails could be tracked above desert scrub.

"I think you've got yourself a dog." Jim laughed. "As soon as you leave here, you'd better search for the largest carrier crate you can find. Put Mystery in it when you aren't around. Even though we think he's five or six, he needs security. That'll keep your house safe when you're gone."

I recalled Jim's telling me on the phone that the woman who'd first adopted him said he'd ripped up her bedding and chewed a hole the size of a watermelon in the middle of her mattress. "He peed and pooped everywhere," Jim had said. "So she returned him to us."

"On the phone, you told me you knew something about Afghans, didn't you?" Jim asked. We'd already been through this, but Jim wanted assurance.

I nodded.

"They're sight hounds," he said, repeating what he'd told me earlier. "They see something and take off."

"I got my previous Afghan as soon as my divorce went through," I said. "I've long been drawn to Afghans. I don't know why. I had my Afghan, Oriana, for years."

Mystery wrapped his legs tightly around my chest, as if to hug me tight, never to let go. He fussed, whimpered happily, and yapped away. The distraction was welcome. I didn't want to dwell on the past, certainly not my bad marriage and divorce.

I looked into Mystery's eyes. "Oh dog, I know you're the one." Tears welled in my eyes. For weeks, he'd been tweaking the telepathic connection, finding my frequency. "I need you—rescue me!" he'd broadcast. "You are mine. I am yours."

I lowered my head, so his cheek pressed against mine. "I am yours, and you are mine—for as long as we're given." By then, I could hardly speak. I hugged him tightly, gathered my wits, and opened my mouth, but the words remained only in thought. *Hello, willful, curious—beautiful—swift-as-the-wind, Afghan. Hello, Mystery, my friend.*

Getting to Know You, Getting to Know Me

On the way home, Mystery positioned himself in the back seat so the rearview mirror framed his face. Every time I looked in the mirror, I couldn't help but see him glance at the scenery on the right, then on the left, and, next, gaze at my face in the mirror.

"So Dog," I began, watching his eyes lock on mine in the mirror, as if to give me full attention. "I want to know how you tune in to me. What's the connection?" He pulled his lips into a smile, not a broad smile, but a knowing, mysterious smile. "I know you think of me as coming to save you from the labyrinth where you were imprisoned." My musings went unanswered. "How did you find your way onto the Stapleton runway?" I kept wondering if his smile might turn downward, if something I said might prompt a change in his demeanor. "Did you escape a carrier crate on a plane? Were you headed to a dog show somewhere? Why don't you have any identification, no micro chip?"

I shifted directions. "You think you're talented, don't you?" I asked. "You *know* you're very skilled is more like it," I added, in a low voice. As wonderful as his aptitudes were, each of his gifts, I knew, could be dangerous.

"My earlier Afghan, Oriana, barreled out of the front door during an early blizzard in September, and got bounced off of five cars on Federal Boulevard. The emergency vet didn't expect her to live, but I took her home, kept laying hands on her, and she made it for fifteen years. Trouble is, she was never all there, sweet but none too bright."

Mystery opened his mouth and yawned loudly.

"I'm telling you this for a reason. I know Afghans. Like you, I hate confinements, both physical and mental."

Mystery smiled, panting heavily. I could almost hear him thinking, "Going home, going home."

"As you know, I'm too independent, too creative to be locked up. By anything, or anyone. I follow the beat of a different drum."

Internally, I heard Mystery remark, "Me too, *ba-dum*. Drum roll, please."

No one had any idea what Mystery's real name was. Although Mystery was a good name, I wanted the idea of mystery to feature less prominently in our life together. Because Afghans have been traced back to Mount Ararat during Moses' time, something Middle Eastern seemed appropriate. I would have to think about the possibilities.

I pulled up in front of the old, two-story red brick building that had recently been converted into nine townhomes. An L-shaped structure, the edifice spanned a corner lot in the tree-festooned Highlands directly west of down-town Denver.

I got out of the car, opened the door to the back seat, and attached the leash to Mystery's collar. The green lawns, the great-leafed canopies of sturdy oak, elm, cottonwood, and maple formed a welcome and cool contrast to Saudi Aurora, as the location of the Afghan Rescue was sometimes termed.

Mystery bounded from the car to the front of my townhome, dragging me along behind him. He acted as if he'd been there dozens of times.

When I opened the door and unsnapped the leash, he glanced at the living room on the right—and bounded up the stairs. I hurried after him. He took a quick look at the guest bedroom, then the study, to which he gave more time, especially the walls lined with books, and pranced into my bedroom. With one great leap, he landed on the bed. Using his front paws, he moved in a clockwise manner and pulled the covers inward toward him at the center of the bed. Seeing his work was satisfactory, he plopped down in the middle, head high and eyes alert. He'd claimed his domain.

"Too bad your throne is only bedding," I said. I walked to my study and pulled down a few books to search for a good Middle Eastern name. Within an hour, I arrived at *Balthazar*, a regal appellation.

Later that day, in the living room, Balthazar crouched on the emerald plush carpet and pounced at me, yapping, as dogs do when they want to play. I reached down to wrestle with him. We both growled and lunged.

Pinning him, my arms wrapped tightly around his chest as he lay on his back, I suddenly found myself overcome by grief. It was as if someone had kicked me in the stomach. My eyes welled up with tears. A deep, convulsive anguish, accompanied by an inability to breathe, overtook me. I'd never experienced anything like this—a foreshadowing of doom that draped over us like a pall.

"Dog, you've got to live a long life. I hope you know that," I said, burying my face in his hair and holding him hard, just as he'd gripped me at the Rescue. I couldn't shake my sorrow, no matter how hard I tried to bring back the playfulness between us. I couldn't find relief. I was tuning in to something awful. I knew it.

Finally, I pushed Balthazar away. I raised myself from the carpet and made my way outside to the calm of the common area in the back. I looked at the roses I'd planted. Big blossoms—deep pinks, blended with reds and peaches, surrounding yellow centers, characterized the flowers of the Chicago Peace near my back door. The Mirandy beside it was bursting with velvety blossoms of burgundy that smelled like baby powder.

The gardens near my unit were always the most luxuriant, not because they got special treatment, as a couple of the residents had once suggested. They didn't. But the phenomenon was curious. My psychic friend Marilyn said, "It's because nature spirits love you." I hadn't seen them—as she professed to have done—but I was open to the idea.

Our Homeowners' Association president and manager had moved to Greeley for work and rented out his townhome. He'd told me he was planning to pay me a salary for the gardening that I did, but I said, "I don't mind. I'm glad to have the three-hundred dollar a year allowance for some plants, fertilizer, peat moss, and so on. I'll still pay personally for some things."

I walked to the back of the yard and slipped out the gate into the alley. I felt guilty for going alone, but I couldn't have the source of my distress with me.

At the street's edge several yards away, the full force of the realization that I was walking out on Balthazar and away from the issues that had come up when wrestling dropped on me. I returned to the house. I was greeted by a huge pile of feces and two wet spots the size of dinner plates on the living room and adjoining dining area carpet.

"Oh Balthazar!" I gasped. He didn't move but stood and watched every move I made. "What a mess." I rushed to the kitchen and grabbed a plastic bag to pick up the feces, which I then tied and tossed in the trash.

Because he'd drunk so much water, I had to run upstairs to the bathroom for a couple of bath towels to soak up the urine. I threw the first one down on one of the spots and stepped on it till it was soaked.

"Why couldn't you have gone on the tiled areas?" I asked. Balthazar had not moved.

Then I used the second towel to soak up the other pool of pee. After that, I scrubbed the spots with carpet shampoo.

He continued to watch. I couldn't tell how he was reacting. "If you have to, the floors in the kitchen and bathroom are far better places than the carpets."

I dumped the soaked towels into the washer, added detergent, turned on the machine, and shut the lid.

Calming myself, I returned to the living room. "We'll work through our anxiety," I said and bent down to hug him. "We'll figure things out."

To push him away, slip out, and leave him alone in the house had made him especially anxious. He was afraid that I too would abandon him. Did he also share some precognitive glimpse into the future which had shaken him as deeply as it had me? That hadn't occurred to me at the time, but with our psychic bond, I suspected that he too had tuned into the future in some way.

"We'll go for a long walk," I said, "but you've got to try hard not to destroy things." I stood up and walked to the foyer for his leash. He followed.

"I don't know how long we have together, my dog. Perhaps not long, if this glimpse into the future proves true," I attached the leash to his collar. "But we have this day, and this night." I bent to hug his neck tightly. "We must take advantage of it. We'll go to a place where you can be free, unconstrained by city traffic and leash."

I drove north to the Clear Creek nature trail just past Regis University. I parked. I opened the back door of the car and unhooked Balthazar's leash. He bounded out and raced along the trail ahead of me, barking joyfully at the air, the creek, the birds, the sky.

Even though I could no longer see him, I found myself sharing his consciousness. I began experiencing what he did.

He spotted a squirrel and gave chase. All of a sudden, the squirrel was staring up into his eyes. Balthazar was on top of him, holding him down with his paws. I felt his heart pounding—racing—terror mixed with the thrill of bagging his game.

Suddenly, the squirrel let out a squeal and bit Balthazar's nose. He yelped and jumped off. The squirrel scampered off and ran up a tree.

I came to the top of the rise and saw Balthazar standing beneath the cottonwood tree where the squirrel now looked down in safety, scolding Balthazar in his loudest, sharpest voice.

Balthazar paced beneath. He barked intermittently. His rebuke was angry but edged with hurt. "You were very bad to run away before Tom had the chance to see with his own eyes what a great hunter I am," he seemed to say. "Why didn't you trust me?"

Like a good sight hound, Balthazar had wanted to hold his prey till I reached him.

Now and then I had seen other dogs catch and kill a squirrel, but there had always been at least two of them. Merely snatching the squirrel wasn't enough for them. They had to eviscerate it too. Not Balthazar. He'd held it and waited for me.

"Balthazar!" I called.

He stopped stalking and cantered over to me, still breathing heavily.

I reached to stroke his head. My heart was pounding. "This relationship," I said, "is going to be very—" I paused, searching for the right word—"awakening."

Cabbages and Kings

For several days, I thought of the dogs that had been part of my life. One of my favorite childhood books was a Little Golden Book, *Mister Dog: The Dog Who Belonged to Himself*, by Margaret Wise Brown. Mister Dog was Crispin's Crispian, a shaggy, funny, shrewd dog who belonged, said Brown, to himself. He found a boy and adopted him. Crispin's Crispian became the boy's mentor, his best friend, and constant companion. Together they made a life.

On every family outing, I would bring this book along, just as the boy and his dog roamed hill and valley together. On a trip to Arizona one winter, I forgot *Mister Dog*, leaving it in a motel room where we'd spent the night. Losing that book was like losing my guide.

After Balthazar arrived, I remembered the magic of this story. I knew I'd met the dog who'd also adopt me and teach me to become fully myself, just as he was fully himself, both of us owned by the other.

On the seventh day of my life with my own Mister Dog, I stopped to chat with my neighbor Johnny. He and his wife, their two kids, and his aged father-in-law lived in a little brick home across the street. Balthazar stood at my side on his leash. Like many of my neighbors, Johnny was quite a character. Everyone knew of his wee-hour-of-the-morning chases after property-destroying kids, his baseball bat in hand, clad in his white jockey shorts, his tee shirt barely covering his belly. I told Johnny my new dog's name. "It's sometimes Mr. Dog, but, formally, it's Balthazar."

"Oh yeah, one of the three wise guys who visited baby Jesus," Johnny said. "When Christmas comes, you can put a robe around Balthazar and a crown on his head. We'll find a baby for a proper visitation." He began to sing in his clear tenor voice. "Oh come, oh come Emmanuel, and ransom captive Israel, that mourns in lonely exile here . . ."

Balthazar, tossing his head back, his hair sweeping off to the side of his noble face, looked up at Johnny and cocked his head, as if listening intently. He opened his mouth as if ready to answer, showing his perfect, long white teeth, not in a snarl, but in a happy manner. Obviously, this dog loved the limelight.

"You're always welcome to listen to me sing," Johnny said, bending down to examine Balthazar's coat of many colors. With satisfaction, Johnny remarked, "Some dog you've got there with hair like corn silk. He must have won all the shows."

Balthazar's eyes brightened even more. He pulled his lip muscles back to show more of his teeth. He opened his mouth wider, sighed dramatically, and then unfurled his tongue, as if he were rolling out a red carpet. For a moment, it hung there in the air. Then, slowly, he pulled it back into his long snout, as if performing some sort of trick.

"He's a happy dog now, a very happy dog," I said. "He's found me, his human companion. And I've found him."

Balthazar began to pull on the lead, signaling that he was ready to go. Because he was strong, I had learned to march after him. He could give me a sore shoulder—perhaps dislocate it—as Jim of the Afghan Rescue had warned.

"Sorry," I said, "Balthazar and I have to counsel someone."

Because I worried about leaving Balthazar in my home alone, I had been meeting with clients there instead of my office.

Darren was a new client whom I was meeting that afternoon. When we set his appointment on the phone the day before, I had told him, "Balthazar, sometimes known as Baltho, or Mr. Dog, will be attending our sessions. Just as I'm still under supervision to complete my therapy training, Balthazar is also training as a therapy dog." I added, "Sometimes, I think he's training me."

Darren laughed. "Dogs are my favorite beasts," he'd said.

When Darren arrived at the door, he was immaculately dressed in a navy-blue pinstriped business suit and elegant black loafers with gold-tipped tassels. Noting the formal attire, I said, "Welcome," and motioned for him to take one of the two winged-back rocking chairs in front of the living room window.

"You must have come directly from work."

"No," Darren replied. "I took the afternoon off."

My face must have given away my surprise.

"I dress like this even on the weekends," he said.

"Well," I began, "I rarely put on a suit and tie, and boy, am I glad to get them off as soon as I can." I sat down in the opposite chair.

Balthazar positioned himself like a king between us. He lifted his head high so that Darren and I had to look at him instead of each other.

Darren's manner, like his attire, remained cordial but rather stiff.

Balthazar looked directly at him and cocked his head to the left and then to the right, as if wondering what was up with him.

"Do you dress like this all the time?" I asked.

Darren nodded. "It goes back to childhood. My mother made sure I put on a set of clean clothes every day that she laid out for me. I could never wear jeans or sneakers, like the other boys."

Baltho edged nearer to Darren. He raised his head so Darren and I couldn't make eye contact. I bent my head to the side so I could see Darren's face.

"I had to wear dress pants and shirt, often a tie. And dress shoes."

Balthazar moaned.

"He seems to be giving you sympathy," I said.

"Thanks Balthazar," Darren said. I thought he would reach to pet him, but he didn't.

For several minutes, I listened to Darren talk about his overbearingly neat and rule-bound mother and his mostly-absent father.

"Do you think your dad was gone so much because he had to work that hard?" I asked.

"No. I think he did it to keep his sanity. My mom wanted to run his life too."

I winced.

Darren continued telling me about his family.

To glimpse each other for a moment, either Darren or I kept moving our head to the side—until Balthazar again repositioned his head directly in our line of sight.

"Dog, please, don't do that," I scolded, pushing his head down.

"It's all right. Balthazar distracts me. I don't like to remember the pain of growing up. I was so lonely. I always had to act perfect and be my mother's *little man*."

I smiled. " Balthazar, will you please move?" I asked. I was tired of his shenanigans.

He got up and moved directly in front of Darren.

Darren seemed about to cry. Just as he reached out to pet him, Balthazar jumped up onto his lap. As if that wasn't enough, he flipped over onto his back. "Whoa," Darren said, holding onto the dog with both hands so he wouldn't fall off. "My suit is slippery," Darren laughed.

Stretching the length of Darren's body, with his back feet now touching the floor, Balthazar touched his nose to Darren's nose and lightly stroked his cheeks with his paws. "He loves me," Darren said, still chuckling.

"He certainly isn't acting very regal," I said. "Some noble royal you are," I muttered, recalling what one of the neighborhood boys had recently said about him. Even though I was trying to sound stern, I also found Balthazar's antics amusing.

"Don't be too hard on him. I envied my neighbors who had dogs. They seemed so happy. My mother wouldn't let me have a dog. She said they were dirty."

"That they are," I said. "But I figure they're worth it. Most of the time," I added, hoping Balthazar wouldn't take that as an invitation to mess things up just as soon as I turned my back.

"I have a hard time opening up. I really need to work on that. I never learned how to interact with people."

"Balthazar seems to know that," I said.

"I feel like a mannequin," Darren confessed, "something my mother dressed and bossed around. I don't feel close to anyone, not even my wife."

"Well, yes," I said, "to be intimate, we have to take off our formal attire and be seen for what we are, imperfections and all."

"The idea petrifies me," Darren said. His affect was flat. I had expected a physical reaction of some sort, but Darren's body and face remained calm. He seemed to have put his mask back on so that he wouldn't feel too much pain.

Balthazar raised himself so he could touch Darren's cheek with his own.

"I think Balthazar's telling you that you can do it, you can open up and find your real self. It's there beneath the facade."

Darren nodded. For a moment, he seemed about to cry. "I wasn't sure if I wanted to see you or one of the other therapists I set appointments with. Now I know. You're the one. You and your dog."

As if to seal the arrangement, Balthazar touched Darren's mouth with his.

"Oh dog, you're getting a little too intimate," I said. Darren didn't express disapproval. "I'm so glad he isn't a licker. At most, you'll get the tip of his tongue, but even that isn't guaranteed."

I turned back to what seemed Darren's central issue. "As far as intimacy goes, I want to point out that you've already made progress. Baltho, the nickname I've given Balthazar, is showing you how to interact on deeper levels. You're doing fine."

Darren laughed. "Well," he said, "he is a dog, not a human." He stroked Baltho's head thoughtfully. "Nicknames are terms of endearment, aren't they?"

I nodded. "We use them for people and animals we feel close to." I paused to let the point sink in.

Darren nodded. "You make a good team. Like you, he's creative."

I glanced at my watch. "It looks like our session is about over. It's been good. Next week, same time?" I asked.

Darren nodded.

I stood. Balthazar and I accompanied him to the door. I smiled down at Mr. Dog, who stood at my right side, his head under my hand. I stroked it. "We'll see you soon."

We watched, as Darren walked down the steps to his Mercedes parked at the curb.

My Diagnostician

Quickly, Baltho had proved a helpful partner in my psychotherapy practice. During the first month, he made clients comfortable. He pointed out problems and solutions that I might have missed on my own. He tuned in psychically. My approach began with reason, to which I added the intuitive, taking cues from him. Together, we made a formidable team.

A new client, Carmen, telephoned for a therapy appointment. She was twenty-seven, originally from Nicaragua, and had been in Denver for only a short time before suffering a car accident. "A truck the size of a military tank rear-ended the little car I was riding in. He injured my neck and spine."

Holding the phone to my ear with my left hand, I reached for a pen and a piece of paper with my right hand.

She added, "I am anxious and unable to sleep. Every night I break into sweats. I fear someone will appear from nowhere to harm me. Sometimes he drives a truck or a car—sometimes he carries a gun or a machete. This time, the blow will be fatal," she said, her voice shaky.

She was verbal. I already had a page of notes. She told me she'd seen a number of therapeutic practitioners for her mental state. "The accident was nine months ago. My body is better but nobody has done my mind a thimble of good."

"Will your insurance permit you to see me?" I asked.

"You are not on my list of approved providers," Carmen said, "but the case manager for the car owner's insurance has agreed to let me see you."

"As long as I get the go-ahead from them, I'll try to help," I said. I wrote down the insurance company's number.

When I called, Carmen's case manager said, "When Carmen gets going, she's like a rat terrier. She grabs you by the scruff of the neck and shakes and shakes till she's worn you down."

"I can't say I blame her. After all, it's her health—her life," I said.

Once Carmen's insurance company agreed to let her see me, I told the case manager, "I don't want to be limited to seeing Carmen for only one therapeutic hour a week. I want to tackle this creatively, without many restraints regarding time or frequency."

When I phoned Carmen to set an appointment, she let me know that she especially distrusted white males of the North American variety because her father, she believed, had been murdered by the CIA. "The system," she complained, "always favors the man, especially if he's a white man from the United States."

"As a white man, my situation is even more complicated," I said, feeling that Carmen was perhaps putting me in a no-win, double bind of "please help me—but you can't." I paused to think. "I've been looked on by those in power as a traitor to my race and gender because I don't lord it over those considered less than me—those of color, women, gays, the poor, and so on. The list is long." I paused. "But I've also been looked on with suspicion by the disempowered because they mistake me for a typical white male," I said. There. Put the double-bind out in the open. See what Carmen would do with it.

"You are different," Carmen said. "I want to see you."

I gave her my address.

"You live in the Highlands. I know it—it's very mixed. That's good."

When Carmen stepped inside my foyer, Baltho pranced up to greet her, just as he did everyone. "My goodness, is that a wolf?" Carmen asked, her pronunciation exaggerated, her cadence slow. Wide-eyed, she drew back. "He is so grand—gigantic!" Every vowel and consonant took on prominence. "His hair is at least as long as a ruler."

I laughed, not just at her reaction but at her way of describing the length of his hair. "The only wolf that begins to look like Baltho," I began, leaning toward Carmen and whispering, as if letting her in on a great secret, "is found in those imaginative drawings for Little Red Riding Hood books. But they don't look like any wolves that I've actually seen. The drawings are clever. So is Baltho. Insightful too. You'll see. Now, don't pull back. Lean forward, Carmen. Reach out your hand," I said, encouraging her to stoop down and stroke Baltho.

With some hesitation, Carmen tried to reach out and touch his head. I was struck by the similarity in Baltho's and Carmen's coloring. Carmen's skin was a warm, dark brown, and her black hair had a reddish sheen. Other colors—grays and blondes—showed too. She too was a brindle.

Baltho looked up at Carmen. He cocked his head and grinned.

She jumped, let out a squeal, and stepped back.

"His face is most hairy," she said. "His nose is even greater than it looks with all his whiskers."

Baltho looked up at her.

"I am fearful," she said, letting out another squeal. She took another big step in reverse.

"You're going to scare him, Carmen. Be comforting. Soothe him with your voice as a mother soothes a child," I instructed in my most comforting voice. "You must help him feel safe and loved."

Carmen stepped forward to try again. This time, she managed to stroke Baltho's neck. Then, slowly, she moved her hand up to his head. "Oh," she began, her strokes elongating from the top of his head down his now-arching back. He stretched, his upward-curved tail extending. "He's so soft. I've never felt a dog with such soft hairs. They are like the hairs of my father. They are dark, with red and black and gray."

"He's a red brindle," I said, "giant sized. His coloring is very like your own. I assure you, Baltho is a dog, a big lovable baby who will soon win you over."

With a nod and a smile, I motioned Carmen with my right hand to go to the living room. "He's suffered lots of psychological damage and needs all the help he can get from people around him." I was consciously attempting to nudge Carmen into a supportive role by projecting her own psychological distress onto Baltho.

"Well, if you are certain," Carmen said, still unsure. She sat in one of the two winged-back rocking chairs near the front window. I sat in the other. Baltho sat between us, raising his head high, and lifting it higher as we talked, so that we couldn't help but see him as we looked at each other.

Soon Baltho inched his way over to Carmen, so slowly, so cautiously, that neither she nor I noticed.

Before we knew it, Baltho had his head in Carmen's lap. He pushed. She felt him leaning into her. He let out a great sigh. Then he lifted his head and looked up at her, those big brown eyes looking plaintive. He sighed and dropped his head down firmly again in her lap.

"He needs you to comfort him."

Carmen began stroking Baltho's head again. Slowly, she moved her hand down his back. "He is just like a child, a human child," she crooned. She was moving past her anxiety, just as I'd hoped.

She had first identified Baltho with her father. Now she was seeing him as a child. If things went well, she would step fully into the mothering role, seeing him as like her own child.

I'd not seen Baltho act the part of a child before. I couldn't have asked for a better intervention.

Carmen began to open up and talk of her experiences in North America. "I know my fears of being killed come not only from the accident but from my father's disappearance. I was only thirteen. I do not think he had been a criminal, but the CIA was rumored to be involved," she said.

I had no reason to doubt her. "I've read of the CIA's shady activities in Latin America and elsewhere in the world."

"The United States is like a great, black octopus. It has tentacles everywhere," she said. "Some therapists think I'm lying," Carmen said. "I know without them telling me. They are poorly informed regarding world situations."

I nodded. "So much depends on our experience, both personal and that gleaned from others," I said.

"North Americans want to think their country always has clean hands." Obviously pained by the thought, Carmen shook her head slowly from side to side.

"For years, I've networked with socially conscious people who haven't been blinded by popular notions."

For the first two weeks, I saw Carmen twice a week for extended sessions. After that, we cut back to once a week, often still for more than one therapeutic hour. Baltho helped me do therapy by placing his head in Carmen's lap and sighing loudly, raising it to look to her for approval, then dropping it down again with a huge sigh of relief. Clearly Carmen's first identification of Baltho's hair with something of her father who was murdered, had opened the way for her familial and then maternal instincts to take over. She was now comforting the dog, who was comforting her in return.

I decided to push the comparisons. "Both you and Baltho are comforting your inner children, or in Baltho's case, his inner puppy."

Carmen laughed. She let out a sigh of acknowledgement. She nodded. "I am again able to feel some happiness."

Along with our talk therapy, which included slowing the car wreck down, replaying and working through each bit, as if a slow motion movie, I suggested we devise some prayers and rituals to dispel the Dark or Evil Forces that Carmen said she felt around her. "In the future, you can draw on these prayers and rituals as you need them," I said.

She decided to invoke the Trinity and the Virgin Mary for protection every morning and night. "I want also to ask for the Archangel Michael, warrior and leader of God's angels, and my father and his mother to watch over me," she said.

"Heck, let's invoke all the angels and archangels, even those whose names we do not know, and the whole host of Heaven," I said.

Carmen laughed. "Yes, it is always good to ask for the best."

"You might like knowing that Mother Cabrini and her nuns used the two units near the alley as their Denver headquarters in the early part of the century," I said. "In fact, the building has been everything from apartment house to tenements in the past. I've even heard that it's been a whorehouse. It was completed in, or even a little before, 1890—making it pretty old for the West."

Carmen nodded. "That is old for a young area of this infant country.

"My friend Marilyn told me she'd seen the spirits of nuns walking in and out of the two units near the alley." I paused. "This was before I'd ever heard that nuns of any sort had lived here. Soon afterwards, I did some checking and found out that Marilyn was right. The nuns must have been with Mother Cabrini."

"Do their ghosts still haunt the quarters?" Carmen asked, her eyes widening. She stroked Baltho's head with more vigor. Her anxiety seemed to be rising. I figured I'd better calm her.

"The only spirits I've encountered here have been those of my grandparents, and my great aunt," I answered. "My grandfather manifested, sitting in my old wooden rocking chair, a few months before he died. He said, 'So long, Tom,' and disappeared. My grandmother and great aunt both appeared to me awhile after they'd died." I paused to remember. "Oh yes," I added, "a high school friend who died in college also came to me in the courtyard out back. I only heard his voice. I saw the others."

"These are common experiences among my people. It is good you do not block them, as many people in your country do." Carmen leaned forward, her eyes opened wide. "Do these appearances scare you?"

"No, I knew who they were. And their apparitions seemed consistent with their earthly personalities, so I had no reason to doubt them." I leaned forward. "I told you I wasn't a typical white male, didn't I?" I joked. "Truthfully, I'm more afraid of the living than I am of the dead."

Carmen's eyes grew wide, and she nodded slowly, dramatically, stroking Baltho's hair as he sighed now and then. "I comprehend."

When I turned in the bill and treatment notes for Carmen's first eight counseling sessions, the case manager phoned to ask some questions. She asked, "Do you believe the Dark Forces and the rituals Carmen and you performed were real?"

"It really doesn't matter, does it?" I asked. "Carmen believes they're real. I get my clients' beliefs working for them."

Carmen, I recalled, had told me that she too had psychic abilities. She also believed it possible to cut the power of the Dark Forces, which she vowed were also after me. "They want to destroy you too," she warned. She straightened up in the chair and shivered, her face darkening, as she turned to Baltho and back to me. "Beware. They want to destroy him especially. He is a path to you."

I shivered. The premonition of his doom returned. Although Baltho still wanted to wrestle, I just couldn't. Every time I did, I tuned into something that made me convulse in grief. Each time, I told him, "Dog you've got to live a long life. Your death will kill me."

I asked Carmen to help come up with some rituals for me to perform. I wanted to keep her involved in the healing process, which naturally extended to others. Her nature was to share what she'd learned, something all of us need to do.

"I shall do so gladly," she replied. In the prayers she gave me, she added an invocation to my grandparents, my great aunt, and my best high school friend, asking them and the Trinity, the archangels, angels, and the entire company of Heaven to protect me. "You should call on the

Virgin Mary too," she added. "You need a good mother who always understands. She desires your excellence."

Taking Carmen seriously was crucial to her improvement, something other therapists before me had seemed to miss—or had neglected to put to good use. I emphasized that truth in my reports to her insurance company.

After the twelfth visit, Carmen's case manager phoned. "In a short time, Carmen has made more progress with you than she made with any other practitioner. That's saying a lot," she added. "We really wondered if she would ever do better." In her report, she wrote that, "His methods were effective, although not conventional."

Allowing Carmen to see me had cost the insurer twenty-three hundred dollars. They'd spent ten times that on other mental health professionals who hadn't been able to get results.

Baltho had certainly held a key to unlocking Carmen's trust and helping her move on. I wondered how much the case manager had heard about my therapy dog. Although I had said little about Baltho, I figured Carmen might have said a lot. She had grown enamored of the dog.

"He is so wise," she exclaimed. "I was fearful of him, but now he seems like my own child."

"Sometimes the big bad wolf turns out to be our best ally, even our partner," I suggested, thinking of the necessity of befriending our Shadow. Only then, does it work with, instead of against, us.

One of my supervisors had advised me to keep my dog away from clients. "He might frighten them." The scene floated into consciousness. "He'll distract you from the business of therapy. If he bites someone, you'll get sued."

"You were wrong, so wrong," I whispered, talking to him in my head. I smiled a big, wide, Baltho grin.

Tweaking the System

Two months after I'd adopted Baltho, the weather turned hot—with afternoons that got into the low hundreds Fahrenheit and nights that didn't go below the mid-seventies. The roses in the common area had started their second round of blooming. Because of the heat, the buds and flowers, especially those of the red roses, looked like someone had turned a blowtorch on them. As a gardener, I knew they would come back in the cool of the fall. But the temporary damage upset me.

During the summer, my therapy training didn't make many demands, but I had a mandatory all-afternoon training workshop downtown. The temperature was expected to peak at a hundred and six degrees.

With careful planning—going out early in the morning and finding heavy shade—or at night—I had been able to take Baltho with me until then. Even if I found a nice shady spot, the car would be too hot for Baltho to stay in. The underground lots suffered heat build-up, staying nearly as warm as outdoors. I checked on the building where the workshop was to be. It was a No Animals Allowed facility.

I had no choice but to leave Baltho at home without me. The dreaded day had finally come.

Suffering no backtalk—the heat made me cranky—I picked up Baltho and carried him to the guest bedroom. There I'd put the jumbo crate that had taken me two weeks to track down. I knew Baltho would never set foot in that room on his own. He knew what was there. With a push, I forced him inside the crate and latched the door.

His bark was so loud, deep, and angry that my ears hurt. Soon he gave that up and tried whining in his most plaintive, high-pitched, ever-weakening, "I'm dying, I'm really dying," voice.

Guiltily, I stole down the stairs to leave. Even with the double brick firewalls between units on both sides of my townhome, I wondered if the noise would be heard by my neighbors. As I drove off, I envisioned the spirits of Mother Cabrini's nuns keeping watch over Mr. Dog for me. Maybe they could calm the savage beast. After all, they'd cared for Denver's sick and needy.

My mind was hardly present at the workshop. I kept worrying about leaving Baltho alone. I'd betrayed him. I knew that's what he thought. "Two creatures who belong to each other are not supposed to betray the beloved," he'd tell me. "Yes, that's what the idealist in us all thinks," I answered in my mind, as if he could hear. "But the experienced soul knows better. We sometimes betray those we love, although not willingly."

Wondering if Baltho had settled down, I kept mentally telegraphing my presence. With my return, I would release him from what he believed to be an Iron Maiden I'd bought for him.

A few days before I chucked him into the crate, I'd tried to prepare him for that fateful hour when he'd have to go into that object of affliction. I had taken him into the guest bedroom and tried to get him to step into the crate, but he wouldn't get near. He knew what crates were for. Confinement. Control. Everything he despised. All the things I hated myself.

I went downstairs for a treat to tempt him. Sensing that he would be fed, Baltho followed close behind. I opened the refrigerator. As I surveyed the contents, Baltho stuck his head in and began nosing around, pushing glass and plastic containers about with his snout. His sniffing was loud, aggressive, as if to take in as many odors as he could. "If you inhale any harder," I said, "you might be able to suck something in, container and all. Right up your nose."

The danger of showing Baltho how to snoop around the refrigerator came to mind. I knew this new ability had lodged in his. He was smart. He was more observant than any creature I'd known.

I pushed these thoughts aside. I had to figure out how to get him into his crate with as little struggle as possible.

Soon, we located some leftover pieces of chicken in a glass baking dish near the back of the second shelf. He really approved of these. He tried to grab one of them just as soon as I moved the other containers out of the way.

Pushing Baltho's nose aside, I grabbed a boneless portion of white meat and a chicken neck, then shut the refrigerator door. "Don't worry, you'll get them," I assured him, as he kept trying to rise up and snatch the treasure from my hands. With Baltho at my heels, threatening to knock me down the stairs, I held onto the railing with one hand and carried the chicken to the crate.

I bent down, stretching to place the neck at the rear. Although I coaxed Baltho to get inside and eat, he still wouldn't go near. He kept trying to swipe the white meat from my left hand. "So the neck isn't good enough. Right?"

Holding my fist tightly, I stooped, reached in, and deposited its contents at the back. I coaxed and coaxed for Baltho to get inside.

Finally, Baltho poked his head in. He spread his back legs to prevent being pushed all the way in—and began devouring every bit of the chicken, moving greedily from one piece to the other.

I got behind him, released one of his legs, and pushed it inside. In response, he spread his other leg further out. He managed to gain some sort of toe hold. I couldn't push him in. Just as soon as I switched my attention to that other leg, he'd push the first leg out of the crate. And we'd start all over again.

"You really love crates, don't you," I said, giving up for the day. "Mastering this trick is going to take time."

Knowing that he was free to go, Baltho pulled his head and upper body out and looked up at me, flinging his head back defiantly. He barked three or four times in his best, and most piercing, deep voice, as if to let me know that he fully intended to have a say in everything that was going on around our house. If he didn't approve, I might as well forget it.

That was why this time I'd offered no fateful food. I just picked him up and shoved him into the crate and latched the door.

Our workshop facilitators wanted us to role play. This was another course in marriage and family therapy. Once again we were to play a family in trouble. We typically found ourselves enacting roles that we'd learned in our own families of origin.

"What part do you want?" Mark, one of the facilitators asked. He'd come to stand directly in front of me.

I hemmed and hawed. I'd only half-listened. I had the sense he'd had to repeat his question. "Sorry," I apologized. "My mind was elsewhere."

Nella, a middle-aged woman from Germany, piped up. I found her friendly but prickly. "He'll play the family dog. That's the part he likes best."

"Grrr," I growled, not too loud, not too long, staring right at her. "You're right. Not that I was the dog in my own family of origin. Well, maybe I was," I said, straight-faced. "But I could easily play the father, the son, or someone else. Not the Holy Ghost, however." I paused, letting my words take hold. "Yes, I prefer the role of the family dog. I get to go around and bark when family members are starting to pick a fight, or lift my leg on the furniture because I'm being ignored. I can express the entire family's distress. I can make a number of points—if only people pay attention."

"He always has to make light of everything," Nella complained, as if asking Mark to scold me. She seemed to think I'd said nothing true at all. "Tom's a goof-off. He acts dumb."

Jack, the head of the training program stepped forward. "Nella," he said, his voice friendly but firm, "You could use some of Tom's playfulness. He often manages to lighten up the heavy situations people are stuck in. He can move families when many can't. You could learn from him. He's been compared to the famous therapist Carl Whittaker by more than one of our faculty."

I wanted to say to Nella, "So there," and nip at her heels. Whittaker was known for his creative provocation. In a legendary case, he treated a family who were convinced their grown daughter was possessed by the devil. She had the entire family under her thumb. As if taking the matter of the woman's possession seriously, Whittaker began adding some bizarre, exaggerated touches to his interpretation of events that he verbalized to the family. Before long, he had the supposedly possessed woman laughing about her weird behavior, with her relatives joining in. By his humorous and exaggerated reframing of the situation, Whittaker was able to move the system toward functionality. The "possessed" daughter had lost her hold over the family system.

I repositioned myself in my chair. More than anything, I wanted to get home to my dog.

When I quietly turned the key in the lock and opened the door of the townhome, I found everything quiet. All my worst fears—that Baltho had died from a heart attack, or managed to choke himself to death on his own spittle or something—rushed into consciousness. I bounded upstairs, taking two or three stairs at a time.

Baltho began to bark. His voice sounded desperate.

"Yes dog, your savior has arrived! Messiah comes!" I called, rushing into the room. I bent over to unlatch the crate.

Whew! A putrid smell hit my nostrils. Baltho was smeared head to toe in feces and urine. The inside of the crate was also smeared.

"Dogs are not supposed to soil their beds, or themselves," I scolded, hauling Mr. Dog by the collar into the bathroom. I made him get into the tub for a bath. "In," I ordered, pointing at the tub.

He knew what he had to do, stepping guiltily inside. He didn't bark. He didn't even frown.

I took the hand-held shower, turned on the water and wet him down. I lathered him with deodorant soap. I let the soap stay on for a few minutes. He liked to get up on my bed and put his head on my pillow, so I hoped this would both disinfect and deodorize him.

The rinse water continued to come out brown. So I kept spraying him. I soaped him up again. And rinsed some more. "Dog, you are such a pain," I complained.

Just as soon as I turned off the water, Baltho jumped from the tub and raced through the upstairs, shaking himself everywhere he bounded. Then, he started running up and down the stairs, still shaking and barking like a puppy, joy overtaking him.

"That's the last time you'll be crated," I yelled. "I would rather have you soil the floors than have to clean out your crate and wash all that off you again." I added, "That is not an invitation to dirty anything!"

To make up for my torturing him that afternoon, I took him for a longer walk than usual that night. I tried to vary our routes, walking for at least an hour—more, if time and energy permitted. He needed the exercise, and so did I. Our long legs were made for great strides.

I drove a few miles west to Sloan's Lake. We got there about eleven and began walking around the perimeter of the park where the lake was. Because it was a weeknight, few people were around. We walked into the park toward the water. I unsnapped Baltho's leash. I'd already made sure the area where I let him loose was large enough for him to run without getting near any street traffic. I knew Afghans. When they spotted something they wanted to chase, they heeded no danger of any kind.

Immediately, Baltho spotted several Canada geese and a clutch of mallards swimming in the water. He raced toward the lake and jumped in. Managing to get within a foot of them, he paddled around and barked joyfully after the fowl. For some time, I watched and listened to his wild abandon. He was an amazingly good swimmer. The joy that he took in simple pleasures was fascinating.

I realized yet again how much I could learn from him. I also needed to let go and enjoy, rather than worry so much about my profession, my clients, my income, my obligations—and everything else under the moon. I never thought of myself as riddled by a Puritan work ethic because I was too creative, but when forced to look beneath the surface, I knew it held me under its foot. Anxiety over what could be, what should be, what would be—had long been my closest companion.

After a half hour, however, I'd tired of standing on the shore and walking the perimeter of the lake, waiting for Baltho to return. "Mr. Dog, are you gonna stay out there forever?" I demanded. I began to call him. "It's half-past twelve. Let's get home!"

Baltho paddled over to the edge and attempted to get out. But the perimeter of the lake was a swamp of deep mud. He got stuck, slipped back into the water, and tried another spot—only to repeat the scenario.

He began whimpering, expecting me to help him.

"Well dog, you got yourself into this mess," I said. "You're going to have to get yourself out."

He made two more attempts. Finally, he pulled himself through the mud onto the shore.

Although I couldn't see him well, I soon realized that he stank of goose droppings. As he neared, I saw that he was covered with slime.

"Dog, how in the hell am I going to get you home? I don't want mud and goose poop on the upholstery of my new car." I had just bought an emerald Mazda 626 LX the week before getting him.

Reaching to pet him, to calm him, I caught my hand, stopping in midair. "I don't pet filthy dogs," I said, withdrawing my hand. Angrier still, I said, "Dog, I should stuff you into the trunk to haul you home. We'll pretend you've just been bumped off in a gangster film."

He adopted an abused dog look, his head hanging, the animation gone from his eyes and mouth. "Well," I said, "there's nothing to do but walk around for another half-hour till you dry, at least enough to ride home in the back seat. You know the treat you'll get when we get there, too, don't you," I said, figuring he'd know I would give him another bath, the second that day.

Meanwhile, I had to pee. I had learned the hard way that I had to keep an eye on Baltho when I peed outdoors. He'd think he had to lift his leg and try to pee alongside me, blending his pee with mine. If I weren't careful, he'd manage to get himself peed on. But, that didn't bother him. Not in the least.

It appeared, however, that Baltho knew better this time. I found a dark spot near some bushes. He stood a couple of feet away. "My guess, however, is you know you're in enough trouble without seeking more."

For ten minutes, we walked around the grassy areas. I checked his hair by putting a finger on his head. It was still soggy, so we walked around the lake. Twenty-five minutes later, his hair looked damp, but no longer soaked. The slime had dried into a damp dustiness. I bent over him and took a whiff. The odor of poop had faded.

We walked back to the car. I opened a rear door. Baltho jumped in. I caught more odor.

At home, Baltho enjoyed another bath at two in the morning.

Getting to bed at two-thirty, I was soon startled from half-sleep by Baltho's feet as they hit my chest. He was hoisting himself up on top of me. "Hey!" I yelled, pushing him away. "What in the heck do you think you're doing? You're supposed to take care of me, just as I take care of you. Instead, you take advantage."

He decided to make another attempt at getting on the bed—but this time more carefully. He chose to stand at the bottom of the bed and jump up on it. Once there, he walked up beside me and dropped down, like a dead weight. He sprawled out, his body paralleling mine, as if his latest torture session had been forgiven. He placed his head on my chest for a pillow. I reached to stroke his hair. He was so soft after a bath. "You smell so fresh and clean," I whispered. He wrapped his leg around my arm, placing his massive paw in my hand. Soon, we fell asleep.

By dawn, Baltho had turned his body perpendicular to mine. That way, he could get a better view out the window. I felt him trying to push me out of his way with his back legs—that is, off the bed.

"You really are asking for it, dog!" I yelled. I reached down and pulled him back parallel to me.

He barked angrily, as if threatening to bite me for daring to move him.

"Mr. Dog, you can be such a pain," I complained. "I know you'll never bite me. But, you raise lots of din. Now, let me get some sleep. And don't you dare wake me till I've slept a couple more hours!" I added. I buried my face in my pillows, as Mr. Dog hid his head between my arm and my chest.

For Every Action

A neighbor in the next block kept a large female German shepherd. He usually had her penned inside a twelve-foot high chain link enclosure at the back of his lot.

I'd heard a bent old man mutter, "Dangerous dog imprisoned in the big house for good reason," as he walked by the house where the dog called Honey was pacing her cage.

Every now and then, I'd see Honey out stalking the yard. Despite her name, Honey remained silent, aloof, and threatening. I tried never to walk by when she was not caged.

One day, as Baltho and I stepped in front of the neighbor's yard, I realized that Honey was out. She appeared to be minding her own business near the back alley.

As Baltho and I moved forward, Honey's ears pricked up. Her back stiffened. Her hair stood along her spine. She ran up to the front of the lot and began to threaten us by zigzagging a few feet away.

Back and forth, back and forth, she paced, silent at first. Then she began to growl, her tail straight out, eyes blazing, lips curled back to reveal front and lower teeth. She was inviting a fight.

Baltho was on his Extenda Leash. At first minding his manners, he soon began to mimic Honey's motions. Honey's aggression heightened.

Zigzagging back and forth, back and forth, they both paced, picking up speed. Honey snarled. Baltho snarled. Honey barked—Baltho barked. His voice grew louder, deeper, more vicious, like hers.

I continued to walk forward, keeping a firm grip on the leash handle, hoping Baltho would follow my lead and abandon the provocation. With a great lunge, Honey reached out and grabbed Baltho's nose with her teeth. The Extenda Leash flew out of my hand. Honey began to run back and forth, dragging Baltho along with her, his long hair going in all directions.

Baltho screamed.

"Let him go!" I roared at Honey. Frantically, I searched for something to bash Honey with—a big rock or two-by-four. Even a shovel. I couldn't find a weapon. "So help me, I'll kill you with my bare hands!"

I managed to get a good kick at Honey's chest. She refused to let go of Baltho's nose. I was afraid to get my hands near her. Finally, I got in another good kick, and Honey let go. Baltho pulled away. He shook his head, coughing, sneezing, blowing blood everywhere—on himself, on me, all over the grass—splattering the sidewalk in red.

I turned toward home and rushed Baltho back. One of the neighbors had witnessed the scene. "I'll stay outside and hold him while you phone the vet," she agreed. She already had Baltho's leash in her hand.

Hurriedly I dialed Dr. Smith, the vet. I assured him that Honey had only gotten hold of Baltho's nose.

"Nose wounds bleed a lot," Dr. Smith said, telling me to go outside and have a good look at him. "Come back and tell me what exactly you found."

I ran outside and took a closer look. Baltho's right nostril was ripped up the side three-eighths of an inch. He was still snorting and coughing and trying to paw and lick the blood spewing from his nose. Blood splattered the sidewalk, the stairs to my unit, the pillars in front—as well as the legs of my neighbor and me. I had a time getting Baltho to hold still long enough to take a closer look, but I saw no other wounds.

Dr. Smith said to wait a few minutes and see if the bleeding stopped. "If it doesn't, bring him in. Swab his nose every few hours with a wad of cotton soaked with hydrogen peroxide to disinfect the wound. Then apply some Neosporin to the area three times daily for a week, making sure to keep his nose clean. If things don't look better in a week, bring him in for a shot and medication."

Even though I hosed down the sidewalk, steps, and walls in front of my townhome, for days afterwards I found traces of Baltho's blood outside. I saw random streaks and spots inside.

But within a week, Baltho acted his happy self again. His nose had healed, although he would always have a small slit up the side of his nostril.

"You know, dog," I said, partly in jest, patting his head, "When I adopted you, I was warned that you demanded an awful lot. That doesn't begin to describe you. Chaos follows wherever you go. It's one thing after another."

On hearing about his latest episode, my sisters and mother suggested that I put up a "No Vacancy" sign in the window. "It's a good thing you're not trying to carry on a close relationship with anyone," Mother said.

"I know," I replied. "I'd have to choose—him."

I talked with the owner of Honey about keeping her kenneled at all times. "She's dangerous."

"No she isn't," he answered. "Even my baby grandchild plays with Honey," he assured me.

"That's taking a big chance."

"No, it isn't. Honey isn't dangerous."

Shortly after the attack on Baltho, some of the neighborhood boys told me they'd seen Honey kill a cat by snatching it off the sidewalk and shaking it to death.

I told Honey's owner what I'd heard. "I'm sure I could press charges against you," I said.

"Honey isn't dangerous," he said, refusing to budge.

I walked away, feeling as if I would soon zigzag along the fence with him.

I began carrying a walking stick on our tours through the Highlands in case I needed to ward off another marauder. Now and then, some free-running dog would rush out of the bushes or around a corner and attack.

One day I forgot the stick. Before I realized what was happening, a Rottweiler rumbled around the corner of an old red brick apartment building and laid into Baltho—growling, barking, and snapping at him with bear-trap jaws. Even though the dog was big and sturdily built, Baltho grabbed him by the scruff of the neck, lifted him off the ground, and began shaking him hard. He shook him and shook, as if to break his neck.

Everything happened so fast I didn't have time to think. I was stunned. I didn't know how to react.

A few seconds later, the Rott's body went limp, all life drained from him. His neck was broken. I was sure of it. Baltho was a killer. He'd had a taste of blood that wasn't his own.

I realized that five of the neighborhood boys had gathered to watch. They ranged in age from about nine to thirteen. I knew three of them—Jose, Antonio, and Juan—from our walks.

"Oooh, Baltho killed Tiny!" I heard someone say, the boys high-fiving each other.

"I told you Baltho would win," Juan chortled. "You owe me ten bucks!"

"Tiny was the devil. He deserved death," said Jose.

"El Diablo of the hood!" Antonio said.

"Tiny attackted us," Jose said. "But not anymore."

The boys bent to put their arms around Baltho at once and hug his luxuriant hair, as if he were their hero. One tried to get him to raise his paw and high-five them.

My mind raced. I thought of my liability. Would the owner of Tiny sue me or demand Baltho be euthanized? You never knew what someone would come up with or how the legal system would treat you.

All of a sudden, Tiny came to.

The boys gasped. "He's Dracula. Get a stake!"

Rising slowly to his feet, Tiny slowly looked around, as if still in a daze. Sheepishly, tail tucked, he managed to lumber off out of sight.

The kids started laughing. They high-fived each other again.

"Baltho kicks ass," said Juan.

"Baltho, you should have killed that devil!" said Antonio.

The boys turned to me. "Let him off his leash. Send him after Tiny. Let him finish that demon off. Please! Tiny is weak now. Baltho, the Afaghan, can kill him, no problem." They chimed in so fast that I could hardly tell who was saying what. Even the two unknown boys were yelling. All pressed in on me.

"I don't think my blood pressure can take it," I said. "We need to go home and chill out." Baltho was panting as hard as I was. I knew his heart was racing too.

The boys said they knew some other dogs "we want Baltho to fight. They deserve death too." Breathlessly, they added, "We'll take bets and split the winnings. You and

Baltho included. We'll be known through all of north Denver. All of Denver and beyond. Into the whole state. Maybe the country! Baltho, the champion! The killer Afaghan!" Again, all of them jumped in so fast I couldn't keep up with them.

Without pause, Juan said, "People will try to shoot him, so you'll have to get a bullet-proof dog-mobile for him and you to ride in."

"Like the Pope's!" Jose and an unknown boy chimed in.

"My brother loves to fix up cars," said the boy that I didn't know. "He can make a bullet-proof low-rider with flashing strobe lights. It'll go up and down and up and down when you push a button. Then all of us can ride with Baltho," he said, his face shining.

"We could even line the dash with fur from the dogs he's killed," I added, in mock seriousness. A picture of the garish—and ghoulish—vehicle flashed in my mind.

The boys nodded. "Great idea!"

"The truth is, guys, I don't want Baltho to become a fighting dog." My manner softening, I added, "He's too good to be turned into a vicious killer."

After some discussion, the boys reluctantly agreed. They were mightily disappointed, but they let us work off the adrenaline by walking back home.

Wrestling with Angels

Baltho lay on his back on the floor beside me, my arms wrapped tightly around him. My nose to his nose, we looked deeply into each others' eyes. Grief overtook me again. This time, we hadn't been wrestling. I felt that I'd been kicked in the gut and weighted with lead.

"Baltho, let's go for a walk," I said, jumping up to find his leash. I knew I couldn't just run off and leave him in the house alone this time. He hadn't acted out for days. I didn't want to do anything to ruin that.

Outside we saw our neighbor, Ann, puttering among the hostas bordering her front porch. The evening was coming on. In late August, nights came earlier. They hinted of the crispness of fall.

When she saw my face, Ann asked, "What's wrong. You look like you've seen a ghost."

"I hope not," I answered. "I'm OK. Really."

She laughed. "I can tell." I knew she didn't believe me. She moved to her front porch and beckoned for me to take a wicker seat beside the one she sat on. "Baltho is such a gorgeous specimen. I just know he was a show dog," she exclaimed, reaching to pet his luxuriant coat.

He sat in front of her. He tossed his head, so his hair went off to the side, revealing his eyes. He panted happily.

"I've just had another experience of stepping outside time as we normally perceive it," I said, relating what had happened.

"I hope you were just experiencing fear over losing what you love," Ann said.

"This was not the first time," I explained. "The first was the very afternoon Baltho came to live with me."

We'd discussed before whether it really is better to have loved and lost, or never to have loved at all. "If we've never loved, the entire experience remains a fantasy," I'd argued.

Ann had said she'd given up. "I'm thinking it's best never to have loved at all. The pain of losing is too great." Only months before, her second husband had deserted her for a hot, young model. The first husband had also dumped her.

"At least dogs are faithful to the end," I said. She was stroking Baltho, so I joined in.

"You know where you stand with them," Ann remarked. "They never pretend to love you and then run off with a bitch with a nicer car."

I laughed, imagining someone running off with a female dog who drove her own sporty little dog-mobile, akin to the one suggested by Juan and the others for Baltho and me. "Although some have proved better than others, we've both had some real dogs in our lives," I joked.

"Some we made the mistake of marrying," Ann replied. Her mood darkened. "I really do hope this wasn't one of your precognitive experiences." She looked at her watch. "Oops. I must get back to my own ball and chain—that is, that big loveable pooch named Choc. His love is forever."

She turned and waltzed toward her front door, singing softly, "Someday My Prince Will Come." Choc was waiting inside for dinner.

I too hoped that I'd not had one of my precognitive experiences. If I were going to dip into what we think of as the future, I wanted to discover good things, happy things that made me feel that God's in Heaven and all's right with the world. Not things that shook me and made me wonder why we had to experience such calamities. I hated feeling that I was living an ancient Greek tragedy where I was trying to outwit Fate.

By then, Baltho was standing, urging me forward. I heard him through my inner senses, though he made no outward noise. He still sat facing me, looking into my eyes. In my mind's eye, Baltho was standing beside me on a cliff's edge. We looked out over a roiling sea with threatening, dark clouds lowering in the sky. I held a sword. He urged me to brandish it in warning, just as he'd learned to tear into dogs that rushed us, threatening our very existence and that of others.

Baltho had called to me over the miles—perhaps over the years—before we'd found each other. To be doglike, to live in the present—regardless of the destruction that might come—was perhaps the lesson that Baltho was trying to teach me.

Eat the food offered. Scarf it down, or savor every morsel. Lap fresh water, even dirty water, if that is all we can find. Walk, with long, proud strides, head high. Swim with the geese and ducks, bark for the sheer joy of making noise, and run like the wind.

Then, when it's time to say goodbye, let go, really let go. Allow the body to fall away and fertilize the grass and the flowers. Permit the soul to ascend where it can run upon the meadows of eternity, perhaps to return and find us again. Or perhaps to wait there for us, with our beloved friends and family—beyond space and time as we commonly perceive them.

Only when we learn to live fully, to embrace what will be—without reservation, without fear—shall the splendor in the grass and the beauty of the flower be ours. Then—and only then.

I took one look at Baltho. He looked up at me. Our spirits had communed. We walked home for a quick bite of dinner and then went out again. We walked and walked, all the way from the Highlands into lower downtown, or LODO, as it is known. Because it was still summer, people were milling around the streets at midnight. Baltho loved the attention people gave him.

"Is that a wolf?" a guy called as we walked across Larimer Square. "No, it's a bear," another man called from somewhere else.

Some people recognized Baltho as a kind of huge and extra hairy Afghan. "Why don't you have this hound properly groomed?" a woman with an English accent asked, walking over to us.

I was puzzled. "He goes to the groomer every other month. I regularly brush and bathe him between groomings."

"I meant to ask, why does he not exhibit a proper saddle?" She stooped to examine Baltho more closely, moving her hands over him.

"I like the more natural look," I said. "The practice of removing the saddle by pulling it out with a pumice stone seems rather barbaric to me."

"You can have it shaved, as some people do," the woman suggested. "He looks rather unkempt as it is."

I shrugged. "I don't have some or all of his heavy facial hair removed either."

"Well, people say England is the land of eccentrics," the woman remarked. She bid us goodbye and walked away.

Further on, others oohed and awed, with more individuals coming up to admire "the magnificent specimen of a dog."

"Yes, Dog, Mr. Dog is magnificent, most of the time," I said. I was glad to hear some positive comments. I wanted to bask in them.

"You call him Dog, Mr. Dog," one well dressed woman in black leather pants with a lace bustier scolded. She and her male friend walked toward us.

"Mr. Dog is a reference to a cherished book from my childhood," I explained. "His name is Balthazar, but I usually call him Baltho."

"He should always be called Balthazar, not Baltho, not Dog, or Mr. Dog," she said. "He's far too special for those terms."

"I hope we can look beyond appearances," I said. "There's a lesson in that, you know."

The woman's companion knelt to check Baltho's sides with his hands. "Don't feed him so much," he said. "You're supposed to be able to feel an Afghan's ribs. He'll live longer if he stays thin."

Baltho was ready to trot on.

With mock seriousness, I said to Baltho, "No more chicken skin or meat fat for you."

Soon we had passed the crowds. "Some people certainly are opinionated," I said. "If we listen, we have to sort out good advice from a lot of crap."

Baltho and I walked up to the gold-domed Capitol, where a number of young men had congregated on the steps and in the parking areas surrounding the building.

"Oh, such a gorgeous dog!" one perfectly coiffed male dressed in an orange silk shirt and burgundy jeans gushed. He hurried over to view Baltho better and pet him. Not a hair on the young man's head got displaced from the jog.

"Yes, absolutely fabulous," his friend, dressed all in white, said, following. He knelt to pet him. The odor of his cologne wafted to my nostrils. It was pleasant, though strong.

Baltho grew bright-eyed, smiled, and stretched, then sat at attention, lifting his paw to be shaken.

"We just walked up from Larimer Square, where we heard how unkempt and fat Baltho looked," I said, laughing.

"Well, you just do your own thing," the perfectly coiffed man advised. He bent to shake Baltho's paw.

"People who can't live their own lives always want to live others' for them," his friend said.

"And persecute them, while they're at it," I added.

The guys looked at each other and nodded dramatically.

I held up my wrist to look at my watch. For four and one half hours, Baltho and I had been roaming the Denver streets. I excused Baltho and me. "We really do have to head home."

"Where's that?" the strong-scented guy asked. His friend whispered something in his ear.

"Over in the Highlands, just west of downtown," I said.

"You are so athletic," the other one cooed. "I love that. You have staying power."

I laughed and bid them goodnight.

At midnight, Baltho and I arrived home. "Well Baltho, Mr. Dog," I said, undressing. I brushed and flossed, then jumped into bed. "I'll sing you a song that'll make you sleep, and you can serenade me." I paused. "No, how about you just listen," I said. "I don't know that you can carry a tune, and I want us to sleep in harmony."

He hopped up on the bed beside me and dropped himself down. He turned over on his back and spread his legs. He wanted me to rub his chest and belly.

Just as my maternal grandfather sang little ditties for his animals, and everyone else within earshot, I sang a little song about a boy and his dog. I made it up on the spot. "Cabbages and kings, we won't discuss serious things. We'll romp and roam and suck the marrow of life."

Baltho planted his head firmly on my chest, so that I would know it was there. "Goodnight, Mr. Dog," I said. I could see his eyes looking up at me in the moonlight. He wrapped his leg around my arm. Soon, we fell asleep.

Enough to Go Around

I'd decided to start the men's therapy group that I'd been mulling since June, when Baltho came into my life. Beginning the first week of September, we would meet weekly in my home. Baltho would move forward with his work as a dog therapist, and I could advance my own therapeutic skills that had been developed throughout my life. As the eldest child in a dysfunctional family, I'd been expected to solve my relatives' problems. The habit of looking for patterns in the texts of people's lives served me well in the reading of literary texts. Most of my college chaplaincy was devoted to counseling. People had always confided in me, seeking my advice.

I'd put out the word, advertised, and spread flyers around town. I'd followed up every inquiry and expected ten men to take part in the group.

The doorbell rang. My client Darren and another man, Mark, stood on the porch. I invited them in. "Sit wherever you like," I said. They positioned themselves on the living room couch, one at each end. A large space stretched between them. This was the first time I'd seen Darren wearing jeans and a light cotton sweater. He had been working on allowing himself to be less formal and more open to others. To reinforce this remedy, Baltho jumped up on his lap and stretched to touch his face with his paws, just as he'd done the first time they met.

Two men, Jim and Sam, arrived, and sat down in chairs flanking the couch. Then came Ben and Tim. They wanted to sit on the carpet because, "It looks so comfortable." The circle had almost formed, leaving the two winged-back chairs and three other dining room chairs open for the other men.

Father Jack arrived without his priest's collar. The oldest of the group by thirty years, he was clothed in navy-blue dress pants and a light blue shirt. He took one of the winged-back rocking chairs, while I took the other.

"The emerald plush carpet and peach walls remind me of Miami," Darren remarked.

We had begun to warm up to one another.

"I really like your Expressionist paintings," Jim said. "Are they originals?"

"Yes, they're originally from an art reproduction shop," I joked. "However, I hauled the little glass water colors by Ivo, a naive artist, back from Dubrovnik. They weighed a ton. I was afraid I was going to break them."

I stared at the gap in the middle of the couch, and said pointedly, "You guys have proven once again that men fear closeness, except when playing football and other sports. Then they can hug and grab each others' asses—even shower together—and no one thinks a thing about it."

The men laughed.

Baltho jumped down from Darren's lap and walked around the room. He poked and nuzzled each man in the group, so that each had to give him some attention. He then positioned himself in front of the vacant spot in the middle of the couch. He looked over his shoulder at Mark on his left, and then looked at Darren on the right. Getting no negative response, he turned around and hopped up into the empty spot that seemed waiting for him. He turned around and faced forward. He sat down on his hindquarters and tossed his head like a proud show dog.

"For those of you who don't know, Baltho is a therapy dog," I said. "I want you to pay attention to his techniques. He's saying, 'See, I'm not afraid to be close, and you guys had better get over it too.'"

Looking across the room at the men's faces, he searched the demeanor of each man, his face more animated than ever. He rolled out his tongue for them, and then slowly pulled it back in.

"Gee, I wish he was human," Father Jack said. A Roman Catholic priest with a shock of white hair, he had face that looked twenty years younger than he was. He'd seen a flyer for the group in a Cherry Creek coffee shop.

Immediately, all eyes turned to him. I said, "I'm sure we all wonder what you meant."

"I'm too old to give a damn what anybody thinks. I've spent all my life giving but receiving nothing for myself. I have no one to come home to, no one to share my burdens. I like men. The anti-gay propaganda blasting out of Colorado Springs in the name of God enrages me. They want to wipe us out."

"Good for you," Dan said. He'd just arrived. "I'm glad you're taking a stand. Religion is so corrupt."

Some of the men nodded.

"I wonder about myself and my own orientation," Dan said. "I'm married with kids. But I still wonder." He paused. "I've got a great wife. She's beautiful, and she loves me unconditionally."

Mark muttered something. He looked distressed.

"Could you repeat that?" I asked.

He shook his head and looked down. I was afraid that bringing up such volatile issues right off the bat would bring an arctic blast, but the men instead began to chat with each other, like old friends. I observed that the men's postures were becoming more relaxed as they felt less isolated. By then it looked as though we were going to have only eight of the ten men I'd expected, but we'd make do.

"Well, now that we're feeling more comfortable," I began, "I'd like each member of the group to introduce himself. I want each of you to give a short outline of your life and tell us briefly why you joined the group."

After each man had spoken, Darren suggested that we'd better take a few moments to concentrate on Baltho. "He also has a story to tell."

After some moments of Baltho's looking around at folks, panting hard but saying nothing, I suggested that I would play a ventriloquist and fill the men in "On the highlights of my small knowledge of his life and greater knowledge of our life together." As I did, my manner and voice animated, Baltho's head bobbed regularly, as if to punctuate pertinent points and the men's reactions.

"He's a male—he's one of us," one of the men remarked.

"Boy, is he," Father Jack remarked, approvingly. He pointed at Baltho's abdomen.

I winced. "He's supposed to be getting past that," I said, referring to the display of his maleness. "Without his testes, his testosterone levels are supposed to diminish over time. They were just removed at the Rescue last spring."

"Damn. Even without balls, he walks into a room and commands attention," Mark said. "I've always wished I could do that. My wife says I have no self-esteem, so I'm always scrounging for scraps dropped by the big dogs."

Several of us laughed. Baltho let out a deep and happy yip, as if to agree. Mark's manner and looks did faintly remind me of a Pekinese—which, as an animal lover, didn't bother me. I noticed that at least four of the men had nodded, as if they knew Mark's issues well. The lack of a strong sense of self—a healthy ego—appeared to be a common theme in people I counseled.

With a heavy sigh, Baltho lay down, spreading himself horizontally to take up the entire center of the couch. Soon, he'd managed to stretch his lower legs onto Mark's lap and his head and paws onto Darren's. Both men could pet him, and he could make physical contact with each of them, while still being able to look out at everyone in the room

I prompted people to talk more about "Our need to feel strong enough in ourselves to let others walk their own paths, while we do what's important to us."

At certain moments, when Baltho felt people were forgetting him, he would stretch, turn himself on his back, and lift his forelegs up to touch the face of Darren, then lift his lower legs so that he could touch the chest or face of Mark at the opposite end.

"He's got the hairiest stomach I've ever seen," Father Jack remarked approvingly.

"He has a strong sense of self," Darren said. "He makes people like him because he has no fear of being himself."

"On that important note," I said, "I suggest we take a fifteen minute break to stretch our legs, go to the bathroom, get some water, and so on."

Mark and Darren had to lift Baltho carefully so they could slip away to the bathroom or kitchen. "We'd hate to disturb him," Darren joked.

When the meeting ended, an hour after the designated nine o'clock ending time, the men remarked on the ease with which they'd made new friends. "Having a character like Baltho around to conduct therapy makes a huge difference," they agreed.

"I've never done well in a group, but Baltho was so funny I soon forgot my fears," Mark said. "I thought I would be threatened by a gay priest and another man who isn't sure about his sexuality. But I don't think I am. Maybe I'm stronger than I'd thought."

"Maybe you aren't struggling, at least in that way," Dan said. "I'm kind of threatened. As you know, I've wondered. Now I have to deal with it."

Tim said he'd watched women bond and share their deepest secrets, "even how they'd consider doing each other."

Many of us laughed.

"Men would be a lot better off if they could do the same," Tim said. "I'm not saying we should actually do it, but it would be more honest if we could talk about it."

"I trust that each of us will be able to explore our issues in the coming weeks," I said. "It's been a great first session where we began to get to know each other and feel secure enough to expose our vulnerabilities. From such foundations, we can build on patterns that have already begun to reveal themselves." I paused, so that my words could sink in. "It looks as though we're going to be doing a lot of work searching for a true sense of self, a major strain of which appears to be becoming comfortable with our sexuality."

"And the sexuality of each other," Father Jack added. I wasn't quite sure how to take his remark, probably because he was so direct about his homosexuality, but I decided not to pick up on it. From our phone conversation, I knew that Father Jack felt isolated and lonely, even though he was very active in ministries to the poor and dying. He was glad that I too had been a minister. "I love God and his church, but I hate the institution," he explained. "They're two separate things. The hierarchy doesn't dare touch me. After all these years, I know too many dirty secrets."

"We need to stop. We have to be able get up in the morning. And," I added, "Baltho and I still have to go for our last walk of the day."

After everyone had left, I straightened up the living room. Baltho and I left for our walk, which couldn't be too long, since it was near midnight.

The night was lovely, balmy, the sky resplendent with stars, even in the city. Baltho would gladly have walked further, but after a few blocks I told him we needed to go back. "We'll take a long walk tomorrow." Two doors from home, we came face to face with man who'd just strode past our front door. Baltho lunged at him. He barked angrily, as if determined to rip the guy's throat out. He seemed desperate to free himself and go for the jugular of another Tiny.

"I'm sorry. Baltho!" I pulled the leash up short, locked it, and grabbed the collar to hold him against my leg. Baltho kept rearing up on his hind legs, trying to break free like a wild stallion. I had no idea what had gotten into him.

The man didn't move.

"He's usually a friendly dog," I tried to explain, gripping the leash and collar tighter so that Baltho, still menacing, couldn't reach the guy. I put my other hand on Baltho's head and pressed, forcing him to sit.

The man moved quickly. A few steps beyond us, he turned around and said, "I kill dogs like yours. Nothing I like better."

I whispered, "It's no wonder he wants to kill you."

I didn't move but waited for the man to walk down the street. I didn't want him to see which unit was mine. After he turned the corner, Baltho and I went home.

As I got ready for bed, I thought about the incident. I'd never noticed the guy in the neighborhood before. He was probably one of the transients who'd just happened to walk through. I figured he'd been drinking, although I didn't smell alcohol. Maybe he was on drugs. No one in his right mind would have invited trouble the way he did. Surely he was kidding.

A few days later, I opened the *Denver Post* and saw a story in the *Denver Section* about a man who had been arrested several blocks from my home. He was charged with criminally abusing a dog. He'd beaten someone's German shepherd with a two by four. Once he'd knocked him down and stunned him, he tried to break his neck.

According to the story, people thought the man was on drugs. I suspected this was same man that Baltho and I had encountered outside our door.

The reporter wrote, "The abuser will probably receive a small fine and no jail time, since animals are considered property in Colorado." I felt my face flush with rage. Those who abuse animals and those who abuse children suffer closely related personality disorders. Young abusers of animals often go on to abuse children. Baltho's insights had been right. "Abusers require mandatory treatment," I said, closing the paper in disgust. "When will we learn?"

Power Trips

I pulled the car close to the west side of the Sam's Club warehouse not far from home. It was mid-September, warm and sunny, comfortable but not hot. A deep shadow extended out twenty feet. I felt safe parking there and shutting off the air conditioning, which I had going at full blast so that Baltho could get cooled down before I left him for a few minutes. I was shivering from the cold inside the car. I checked my watch. It was ten-seventeen.

I glanced back at Baltho, who was sitting attentively in the back seat, his head up, his eyes alert, panting happily. I hit the switches to roll down the automatic windows a third of the way and turned off the motor. "I've got to pick up a few things. Stay calm and don't exert yourself. If something happens to me, somebody can stick his arm in and pull the lock to open the door and free you."

He tossed his head back as if to say, "Nothing bad is going to happen. Stop acting like a hovering parent."

I sprinted around to the entrance at the front of the building, grabbed a basket, and hastily made my way down the aisle, snatched some toilet paper, paper towels, a gallon of skim milk, and a big container of cottage cheese. I looked at my watch. It was ten-thirty. Not allowing myself time even to look around and see what was new, I hurried to the check out. I didn't know how long the shade would last. Even then, the car might heat up and cook my dog. I knew the warnings and wasn't about to take a chance.

Paying the clerk, I again looked at my watch. I'd been away for twelve minutes.

I hurried outside to the corner of the building. The shade still covered the far edge of my car. An animal control vehicle was parked beside it. A female officer with stringy blonde hair stood at the back window, peering inside at Baltho. He was standing in the back seat with his nose through the open space, looking back at her. From the sounds he was making, I knew he was getting a good whiff of her. She was probably reeking with the odors of many animals.

I called out to the officer. "Hey, I'm right here! I ran into Sam's Club for a few items. The dog's fine. I've been gone for thirteen minutes."

Breathless, I neared. The officer moved forward to block my entrance to the driver's door. Her complexion was ruddy, and the pores of her skin large. "Someone reported a dog left alone in a closed car for over two hours and showing signs of heat prostration," she said, her voice calm, firm. Her face was set. She was out to show me she was a strong woman fully in control.

I tried to move to my door to unlock the vehicle and let Baltho out, so he could get some fresh air and cool down.

The officer still blocked me. "Why did you leave this dog alone in a hot car?" she demanded. "Dogs should not be traveling around in cars anyway. They belong at home where they're safe."

I kept making large, sweeping signs from my chest outward with my hands, motioning for the officer to move back. "I want to let Baltho out," I said.

She seemed oblivious to that fact that the interior of the car was heating up and Baltho was panting more heavily. She went on warning me that cars quickly become ovens, even with the windows rolled down. "Children and pets regularly die in vehicles while waiting for someone to rescue them."

"I wonder how many dogs and children are suffering heat prostration right now in this—or in adjacent parking lots—while you lecture me about facts that I'm well aware of," I huffed. Thinking that changing my approach to a more understanding one might help, I said, "I realize, Officer, that you have no way of knowing that I'm telling the truth—and that I'm a responsible pet owner. But I am. I'd been gone only thirteen minutes."

Baltho panted more heavily with each passing minute. He seemed excited because he was being talked about. He was noticing my distress as well.

The officer refused to listen. She fiddled with her note and ticket pad. "You should not be taking your dog with you in the car," she repeated, still blocking access to the door.

"Look, you keep warning me about things that I am very well aware of," I repeated. "I am a responsible pet owner. That's why I parked here in the shade of the building, twenty minutes ago. It was only thirteen minutes when I returned—"

"You were gone for over two hours," the officer said. "We've got witnesses. You can be arrested—and thrown in jail—"

"Look," I said, with one great push. Now, the officer's body was out of the way. I stuck my key in the driver's side lock, and turned it, which opened all four doors. "My dog is in the car getting hotter and panting more heavily, while you're going on and on about things you know only by hearsay. Now, I am opening the door and letting Balthazar out. If he dies from heat prostration, it's your fault for blocking my way. You can be sure I'll bring a lawsuit and have the media all over you like flies."

She stopped blathering.

Baltho jumped out and looked up first at the officer and then at me, and back again, as if to check out the situation.

I reached down to feel his hair, ruffling it. It was still cool, as was his nose. I pointed this out to the officer, urging her to have a go. "If he'd been left in a hot car for hours his hair would be hot now, wouldn't it?" I said, trying not to let my anger flash out at her.

She resisted bending to feel his hair, even though Baltho straightened and looked right at her, as if to invite attention. My hand was touching him in various places, noting the coolness of his hair in all areas. "Feel him!" I commanded.

Finally the officer felt Baltho's hair herself. While she said nothing, it was obvious that he felt cool to her too. Her hand ran all over his body, while he stretched and looked most pleased with himself and all the attention that he was drawing.

"Your refusing to listen to me and blocking the way so that I couldn't get to him has caused both him and me a lot of stress."

"We had a complaint," the officer repeated. "Animals are better left at home than being hauled around with their owners. People get into accidents with animals in the car. They get tossed out."

"Who, the animals or the people?" I asked. Rather than saying what I really wanted about the growing corruption of America showing up most clearly in people in positions of authority, I held my tongue.

The officer looked a little ruffled.

"No one who knows me would ever accuse me of being irresponsible or not caring deeply about my dog," I said, lecturing the officer. I opened the back door and told

Baltho to get in. "You need to get home and get inside where you will be safe from all harm."

"Are you talking to me?" the officer asked.

"So be it," I remarked.

The officer grabbed her ticket book, and before I could get into the car, wrote me a warning ticket. Officiously, she handed it to me.

I took the piece of paper, threw it on the seat next to me, and drove off. If I hadn't believed that she performed a valuable service on some occasions, I would have called the animal control office and lodged my own complaint against someone so in love with power that she couldn't—or wouldn't—see what was smack in front of her.

Travelers

It was late September, and the day was crisp. The doorbell rang. I opened the front door a little to talk with two Jehovah's Witnesses, an older woman and a child. The woman held the wrought iron security door open with her rear end.

Baltho was quite interested in seeing what they had to offer. He used his head and neck like a horse to force the door open wider and nose his way further into their midst. Soon, he had his front paws on the steps. The Witnesses were forced to pet him.

A boy running down the opposite side of the street caught Baltho's eye. Baltho pushed his way through and dashed after the kid. Continuing to gallop down the street, Baltho stopped suddenly. He glanced back at me and gave out a couple of loud, high pitched barks, inviting me to follow.

Quickly excusing myself, I left the Jehovah's Witnesses on my stoop and dashed off after Baltho. He thought we were playing a game. As I pursued, he'd stop for a moment and look back, teasing and inviting me to come, while giving me the opportunity to catch up. As soon as I'd get within ten feet, he'd start off again, then stop, a half block from me, snooping around until I got in range. Then he'd dash off again, head high, yelping into the wind as if only too glad to have a running mate. I kept worrying that he'd run out in front of a car and get hit, a repeat of what had happened to my first Afghan, Oriana. She'd taught me the dangers of living with a sight hound.

Several blocks later, Baltho ran up to some boys playing outside in their front yard. I yelled that he was friendly and wouldn't hurt them. "Try to get hold of his collar!" I called, running toward them.

One of them grabbed the collar and held on. But, just as I neared, Baltho shook free.

"Baltho!" I called, as he ran down the street again, this time with me and three boys chasing him.

He neared another group of boys.

The boys with me yelled, "Grab him!"

"Don't let him break free," I called.

"He's strong! Really strong!" they called.

"Hold on tight!" I yelled.

This time the technique worked. Baltho was surrounded by one boy who held his collar, with the others holding him by the hair.

I caught up to them. I recognized Jose and Antonio. Juan had Baltho's collar and turned him over to me. "He's so strong—and tricky," they exclaimed.

I nodded and thanked them. With my hand tightly grasping Baltho's collar so he couldn't wiggle free, we walked toward home. He was in high spirits, cantering, and panting like a winded horse.

So was I. My heart threatened to jump out of my chest.

Before I knew it, Baltho pulled his head out of his collar and ran off again—so fast that I knew only the general direction he headed—east. I chased after him, calling and calling. But to no avail. I was sure he'd deliberately given me the slip so that he could roam as long as he desired. He wasn't about to be caught this time.

I spotted Juan, Jose, and Antonio and shouted to be on the lookout for my runaway dog.

"Oh no!" Juan and Jose roared. "You let him get away!" they exclaimed, almost in unison. Antonio shook his head and clucked.

I didn't know what to say. "I don't even know where to look. He ran so far that I have no idea where he's gone. I think he was running down toward Our Lady of Guadalupe, but that's no guarantee of where he is now."

I paced the neighborhood for a good hour but saw nothing. No one that I came upon had had seen him.

Finally I walked home, hoping, and praying, that he would be protected from harm. I worried about my house. We had wrought iron bars on all our back windows for a reason. Burglaries weren't uncommon.

The Jehovah's Witnesses had politely closed the front door, leaving a couple of tracts in the security door. It appeared that no one had entered the house. Everything looked intact. I didn't have a lot that was valuable, but my television, VCR, and stereo were still in the living room. I raced upstairs. My rosewood with brass inlay jewelry box from India still sat on my dresser. In it were my three silver rings inlaid with malachite and the opal ring with two little diamonds that my mother had made for me when her mother died.

An hour later, the doorbell rang. Juan had his arm around Baltho's neck. Jose and Antonio, panting, stood beside the dog, touching his sides gently. "We caught him!" they said. They looked exhausted.

The boys were muddy, and Baltho was knotted with burrs. Lifting his head high, Baltho looked at me, then at each of the boys. He seemed most pleased with himself, not a bit repentant—as if he'd not only had a good romp but had invited friends to come home with him. For a moment, it occurred to me that Mr. Dog was building his family. Get out the big soup pot and go to the garden for vegetables, I thought. We have a chicken thawing in the refrigerator.

"Baltho was checking out the ditch by the freeway," they said.

I noticed how ragged the boys' jeans and shirts were. I wondered if they had torn them trying to rescue Baltho. "Did you tear your clothes?" I asked.

"No, these are our old clothes," Antonio, who said he was going by Tony now, answered. "We play in them."

"Let me see if I have some cash," I said. I reached to pull my wallet from my back pocket.

The boys shook their heads. "We don't want money," they said, almost in unison. They looked down at their feet, as if ashamed.

"You boys helped me. And this very good dog who was very bad made it back home safely because of you. He might not have otherwise."

"We don't need money," the boys insisted.

I tried to hand them a twenty dollar bill. But every one of them refused.

"OK, how about if I give you this ten so that you can buy yourselves something to eat?" I held the bill out to them.

They looked at each other, hemmed, and hawed, shuffling their feet.

Finally Juan said, "Okay," and the other two boys agreed. They helped push Baltho inside.

"We love Big Macs and fries," they assured me. They flashed big smiles. A McDonald's had recently moved into the neighborhood to rival the many Mexican and Italian restaurants. The boys had made up their minds. Fast food had won them over.

Tricks and Treats

In early October, I joined a group of psychotherapists headed by John Gold. A prominent Jungian therapist whom I had consulted about finding a supervisor months before had recommended Gold. "He's creative and a maverick—like you," she said.

On October 30, Gold phoned to invite me to lunch. "Everyone who's joined the practice in our new offices is celebrating. No Halloween costumes though," he added, "even though it's the season. The group is like an accordion. Sometimes it contracts. Now, it's expanding. We're going to make music again."

"That could be fun," I replied. Interested in art, literature, culture, and world travel, Gold also possessed a playful side, all of which I appreciated.

"Be sure to bring Baltho," Gold added. "I've got a real treat in mind. Put him on a regular leash, no Extenda Leash this time."

I looked at my watch. It was noon. Gold had given me an hour's notice. Not unusual for him. Sometimes he'd call, demanding that I get there within a half hour. Only the week before, I had been washing windows when he called and demanded that I get into the car to rush to my scheduled supervision. "I didn't schedule a supervision," I'd replied.

"Yes, you did," he'd insisted. "I have you down for two o'clock. I just looked in my book. It's two-fifteen. We'll make it two-thirty. That will give you thirty minutes, if you step on the speed."

"Fifteen minutes to get there!" I exclaimed. "Are you crazy?" I realized that I'd pushed so hard with the wiping towel that I'd broken the window and driven glass into my palm. Still, I made it, my hand bandaged up, within twenty-five minutes. Gold knew too well how to get what he wanted by guilt, prodding, confusing his opponent—or the brute force of his overwhelming ego and place in the community. He knew that he could push me pretty hard, and I'd comply—even after lots of resistance. I didn't want to take the chance of having him go after me. He could be a formidable enemy.

This time, I didn't resist. Gold said we'd have fun. His manner was playful. He didn't seem manipulative, as if he was looking for a supervision payment.

I put the phone down, packed up Baltho, jumped into the car, and headed to the offices in Cherry Creek. It was a trendy upscale location with lots of boutiques and little shops along tree and flower-lined side streets.

At the door to our suite of offices, Gold greeted me and Baltho with a devilish grin. He called Mr. Dog over to him and pulled out an orange "Dog in Training" vest that he placed over his back like a saddle. With a grunt, he knelt to buckle it underneath. He reached for the white cane resting beside the door frame. "Do you think I should carry this cane or just roll my eyes around like a blind man?" he asked, managing to stand with the help of the cane. "I'm thinking the cane might be overkill."

A hulk of a man, Gold stood and took Baltho's leash in his right hand. Rolling his eyes around in the sockets, he took a practice walk around the outer office and down the hallway. He would almost trip now and then, as if trying to get used to letting Baltho lead him.

I also rolled my eyes, but not because I was playing blind. I wondered if Gold's plan wasn't a little too creative.

Gold barked to his wife, Emma. Her office door was closed. He kept calling until she opened it.

"I told you I have a client until one, or a little after," she said, her voice firm, her volume soft. She was a middle-aged blonde, a third of her husband's size. Emma was careful not to open the door more than a few inches. I couldn't see who was inside. If Gold had been in her shoes, he would have swung open the door and introduced everyone in the office to his client, even hinting of her problems, which, if juicy, he would elaborate on later.

Gold pulled back and sputtered something. He was ready to go. "We'll do your supervision over lunch," he told me.

"You didn't say anything about supervision on the phone. I've told you, I don't need supervision every week. I don't have enough clients to warrant it."

"If you listen to me, you'll have a big practice, like Marty. This is the right location. He got his life turned around because of me. Look at him now. He even works out every day and dresses to the nines. Clients beg to see him, especially gay men."

"I don't want a big practice," I replied, repeating what I'd told Gold several times already. "I have other interests, such as writing and teaching. I don't intend to give them up."

"But you haven't taught for several years," Gold said.

"As you know, I intend to get back in. That's why I keep up with my scholarship and writing. When my Milton book is published, I hope to get a professorial post."

Several of the people in the practice had begun to suspect that Gold looked at his supervisees as cash cows. As a supervisor, he couldn't legally take a percentage of our income, but he could charge us rent for office space, make us contribute to office expenses—paper, computer equipment and upkeep, secretarial staff—and charge for supervision—all for the privilege of being part of his growing and prestigious counseling group. "Besides, I told you, I don't like to do supervision over lunch. You, for sure, don't listen when you're eating."

Gold gave me a hurt look. "You can be very cutting," he said.

"You know it's true," I said, refusing to be cowed. It had become apparent that he would run over me if I didn't brace myself and go after him in return. "Even at the best of times, you don't listen well, and, when you're eating, you're too busy enjoying the food to pay attention to anything else. You told me we were going to have lunch and have fun. This is becoming something different."

"I refuse to talk about it any further," Gold said. "You're hurting my feelings." He acted as if I'd cut him to the quick.

"I don't need extra calories," I said. "I try to eat light lunches with lots of vegetables, ones I prepare at home. That way I know that I'm getting healthy, low-fat meals, with mostly complex carbs. When I go out to lunch with you, you always want big, gourmet meals, with lots of butter, creams, fine sauces, and lots of calories."

"Don't tell me you don't like gourmet meals," Gold retorted.

"Of course I do. But they aren't healthy, certainly not with my metabolism. I've never handled fats and refined carbohydrates well. Such diets make me obese and give me a sugar high."

Gold harrumphed. "It's new upscale restaurant for health-minded gourmets. You and Emma will find it wonderful, I'm sure." He handed Baltho's leash to me and turned. He walked away, back to his office. He farted and shut his door.

I couldn't go into the office that I shared with another therapist because someone was using it. I walked to the waiting area and sat down. I dropped Baltho's leash so that he could do what he wanted. As long as I kept an eye on the entrance door so that he couldn't slip out, he would be fine. He wouldn't go far, but he would explore.

Helen, our secretary, commented, "He's got everyone waiting for him again." She was an old friend of mine who needed a job. I sincerely hoped that finding her this one wasn't going to prove a mistake. "Gold's got some new project going on," she continued. "He's on the phone with the head of the State Regulatory Agency right now. I suspect it's another scheme. He's flattered Mo into being a guest speaker for his ethics classes, greasing the palm again, in one way or another."

I laughed. "You don't know what he's plotting?"

"I'll probably find out. He's not known for being tight-lipped." Helen said she wasn't going to lunch with us. "From what I can tell, no one but Emma is going with you."

"I thought everyone was celebrating."

"Bigger braggadocios with brassier balls are not to be found," Helen replied.

Emma Gold's office door quietly opened. Out walked Marsha, a client, followed by Emma. Regardless of confidentiality laws, Gold had informed the entire office of Marsha's bitter divorce proceedings. "I had to take away the gun that she'd bought for shooting her husband," he told everyone who'd listen. Gold liked to take it out of his desk drawer and brandish it for all who expressed even slight interest. He thought it quite a trophy. "I've got the bullets. I took those away too."

Emma asked, "Where's John? I'm ready to go.'

With Emma present, Gold would behave. I would find something on the menu that was healthy and not loaded with calories.

Gold soon joined us. Off we walked down the street. Baltho played the dog in training, and Gold rolled his eyes and stumbled now and then. "If I fall I will have to sue the city for permitting uneven sidewalks," he muttered desperately, then laughed.

We walked into a new French restaurant. The tables were set with white table cloths, candles, fine white china, and crystal stemware. Gold called out, "Service, Waiter!" His manner and voice smacked of need. "Could you please help us," he said flailing his left arm like a drowning man.

"I doubt if anyone thinks you're drowning," I said.

"I'm blind—my dog is only in training!" he cried.

People stared, admiring the beautiful Afghan. "I've never seen such a marvelous beast, with so many colors," an older man remarked.

"And in training," one smartly dressed woman with white hair and huge gold earrings said. She stood and approached us. "I've heard Afghans are not at all easy to train."

"Oh, this one is very intelligent," Gold responded, loud enough for all to hear. "He was a show dog, but he changed careers at midlife. Please, do not pet him. He must become bonded with me, and me alone," he said, a worried look crossing his face. His eyes moved uncontrollably for effect. The woman apologized and backed away. I was surprised that no one recognized Gold and his wife. But if they did, they chose not to tip off the restaurant staff.

Baltho, the Dog Who Owned a Man

We were led by a waiter to an elegantly laid table in the middle of the restaurant. The place was starting to fill up. I was glad that I'd worn dark dress pants and a nice shirt, although a jacket to accompany the outfit would have been appropriate.

I would have to keep a close eye on Baltho so that he didn't reach over onto our table and snatch something that smelled good, or over onto one of the neighboring tables, and really embarrass me.

Baltho sat down between Gold and me, his eyes surveying the people, the tables, and the food. He looked very happy. After all, he was the center of attention. Well, he and Gold were.

"What a beautiful Afghan. I've never seen one this big or with such a heavy, beautiful coat,' the waiter said, kneeling beside him. He did not touch him. After warning the waiter, "Please, do not pet him," Gold added, "He also helps Dr. Watson conduct therapy. My group is conducting important research on Afghans as therapy dogs. It's very cutting edge."

Emma Gold, as always, managed not to reveal anything untoward in her manner or face, remaining pleasant and professional at all times.

"Dr. Watson may look rather startled or concerned," Gold explained, his eyes still moving like marbles in a jar. "But he tends to worry too much."

If my face gave away what I was really thinking, well, Gold covered those bases too.

"Could you please have the chef make up a special *plat de jour* for Baltho?" Gold asked. "Something of simple elegance. No onions. They're toxic to dogs, you know."

"I'm sure we can come up with something," the waiter responded. "Would you like his plate to be served with yours?"

Gold glanced at his wife, then caught himself and darted his eyes back and forth and up and down again and again. Emma remained straight-faced but shrugged slightly.

"That's probably best," I said.

I couldn't imagine that no one knew Gold was just pretending to be blind. But, I remembered one of his favorite observations, "People believe what they want to believe. Or what others want them to." He would no doubt use this experience to lecture me on group dynamics and P. T. Barnum's well known adage that a sucker is born every minute.

Baltho remained a perfectly behaved dog, even after the waiter presented his plate to him—deboned chunks of chicken breast with sides of fresh asparagus spears and a mound of cooked carrots with an orange glaze.

As soon as the plate was set on the floor, Baltho put his head down and began sampling the chicken, quickly moving to the carrots, back to the chicken, then to the asparagus, and back to the chicken, which he obviously liked best.

"He has wonderful table manners," the woman sitting at a table on my left remarked.

"I've never seen them before," I said, laughing. "This dog is full of surprises."

"It's the atmosphere," Gold added, fumbling for his water glass, spilling a little on the table cloth for effect.

"You could take some lessons," I said, a barb of criticism making its way through.

By the time Emma and I had taken two bites, Baltho had cleaned his plate and was looking over at my plate, lusting for more.

"You've awakened his appetite," I said.

"I have a way of doing that," Gold remarked. He had wolfed down everything on his plate and was reaching over to taste food from both my plate and his wife's with his fork and with his fingers.

"For a blind man, you certainly know where every morsel of food is," I remarked.

"It's the radar that all blind people develop," he explained, scarfing the last of the bread. He opened his mouth to call the waiter over and ask for more bread and olive oil. He spit out a glob. It landed on the table.

Baltho leaned over and snatched a piece of beef from the plate of the woman who had just complimented his behavior. If she noticed, she chose not to acknowledge it.

Although I wanted to scold him, I thought I'd better say nothing. Instead, I pulled on Baltho's leash and stepped on the excess strap. He couldn't move far.

I glanced at Gold, who'd noticed what had happened. He nodded, raising his left eyebrow slightly. Then he began rolling his eyes again and looking rather desperate. "Waiter!" he called, catching another waiter's attention. "Are you our waiter?" he asked, fumbling to touch him. "You don't smell the same," he said, fumbling along his thigh.

"No dear, this is someone else's waiter," Emma explained. She was so used to her husband's games that they no longer ruffled her.

"You'll do," Gold said. "Would you bring our guest of honor a bowl of those nice rosemary potatoes? He's still growing and needs more food." Gold continued to move his eyes as if they didn't belong to him.

Even though I was embarrassed, I wanted to laugh. "You want more potatoes, don't you," I said.

"I'll help him eat them," Gold said. He wasn't fazed by anything.

Lunch finished, we walked back to the office. Gold told me he wanted to make sure that I'd learned from this supervision.

"That was lunch," I corrected, as Baltho sat down. I took off the Dog in Training vest and put it on Gold's chair. "I told you I don't need frequent supervisions."

"People will do anything to keep from acknowledging that they were duped," Gold reminded me. "They want to keep up the front, especially educated people, who ascribe to the veneer of civilization."

"Yes, if they'd been rabble they'd have yelled and set upon the beast, stabbing him with their forks," I said. I was hoping Gold would notice I said "the beast," not "Baltho." I wanted to stress the ambiguity as to whom the rabble would have set upon.

"No," Gold responded, pausing for emphasis. "They wouldn't have been eating in that restaurant." Gold turned to the mail on his desk. "If the embarrassment goes to the other person, however, people are eager to point out the truth." He picked up a letter and opened it. "Don't forget to leave your supervision fee before you go," he said. Noticing the silence as Baltho and I walked away, he called, "I'm teaching you important lessons. Teaching in a very creative way, you'll observe."

Tis the Season

One crisp but sunny late afternoon in November, Baltho and I walked from our Highlands neighborhood into lower downtown. We passed several shops. Many were decorated for Christmas with old-fashioned wreaths, bows, antique dolls, and wagons. Some shops displayed Christmas trees laced with garlands of popcorn, hand-painted ornaments, and electric lights made to look like candles.

We paused outside a designer boutique. A blonde, middle-aged woman, dressed in a winter-white suit, opened the shop door. She walked out to meet us.

"I've seen you walk by a few times," she said. "Do you live in one of the lofts around here?"

A medium-sized, blonde Afghan with a black mask peered out the store window at us.

"No, we're in the Highlands."

"That's a nice walk," she remarked, introducing herself as Jeanie Jerome. "Do you walk miles every day?"

"We try to, but we take different routes. That way we don't get bored."

She invited us in, introducing us to her Afghan, Shehera (she spelled it for us). "I notice you also say *we,*" she remarked. "People wonder if I have an invisible friend. My dogs are my companions. I wouldn't dream of going anywhere without them." She told me to let Baltho off his leash. "Shehera and he can enjoy each other's company freely that way. I hope you show Baltho. I show Shehera."

"No. It's too much trouble. Besides, he's a rescue, so I don't have any papers." I told her the story. "I really don't know much about him."

"He's a huge, beautiful specimen," she said, kneeling to examine him. "Europeans call Afghans like this *European Afghans*. They favor them. You see them in upscale Parisian restaurants all the time. They eat on special plates, sometimes at the table, sometimes on the floor." I recounted the incident with the Golds. She stroked Baltho's head and pulled back his gums to examine his fine, white teeth. "I wonder if he was accompanying a European traveler when he got lost." She asked Baltho, "Can you sit?"

Without hesitation, he sat oh-so-regally, and then turned his head side to side, as if expecting accolades. But the store was empty, except for Jeanie and me. She mentioned some prominent names around town and asked if I knew any of them.

I shook my head. "I recognize some of the names, but I really don't have important connections."

She turned back to Baltho. "He's such a handsome dog and so well trained. I'd be willing to bet he's a champion."

"He's on his best behavior right now because he doesn't know you," I joked.

Jeanie laughed. "Afghans are like that. Much smarter than people think."

"He's never too bad, I must admit."

Baltho decided, as if on cue, to walk over to the twenty-foot-high Scotch Pine Christmas tree festooned with clear lights, gold ornaments, and white ribbons. He sniffed and looked up.

"Be careful, Baltho," I said. "He's usually very graceful and never knocks anything over, in my home or elsewhere," I explained, still watching.

"He's fine. Shehera explores the store all the time," Jeanie assured me. "I've had three Afs in here at once, and they were all well-behaved."

Jeanie got up. "You'll have a glass of champagne, won't you," she said, reaching under her counter for a bottle. Behind her were autographed pictures of people she'd mentioned earlier. She was often standing or seated beside them.

I watched Jeanie pour. I glanced again at Baltho and Shehera. Like two dogs exploring a forest specimen, she was squatting beside him, and he was lifting his leg on the trunk.

"Baltho!" I yelled. "Jeanie, they're not on their best behaviors," I said, my voice low to express my embarrassment.

She laughed. "They're marking territory. It will clean up. I've had worse, believe me."

She walked over to the tree, as the lights started shorting. Sparks flew, and bulbs popped. Then all the lights in the store went dead. The emergency power came on, giving things a dim, yellow glow.

"There's a fuse box in the floor beneath the tree. Their pee must have blown a fuse."

"I'm sorry. I never thought Baltho would do that," I said, feeling red-faced.

"Don't worry about it," Jeanie said. "I invited you in." She went behind the counter to get a roll of paper towels. "I'll replace the fuse when things dry out. It's closing time anyway."

She pulled off some towels and handed them to me. She bent down with another wad in her hands. "I've lived among dogs all my life. I've even had two Afs decide to mate in a store full of people. That was some sight." She laughed.

I helped to wipe up the floor. Afterwards, I made some excuse about getting home. Regardless of Jeanie's assurances, I was still rather embarrassed. I hooked Baltho's leash back on his collar and said goodbye.

Although Jeanie told us to stop in whenever we were in the neighborhood, I wasn't sure how soon we'd do that. "I hope you and Shehera haven't done more damage than Jeanie thought," I said to Baltho as we walked home. It was getting cold. I hadn't worn a jacket or a sweater, merely a plaid shirt and jeans. "I know Jeanie invited us in and told me to unhook you and let you explore. But what in the world were you thinking?"

Baltho made no noise. He trotted beside me, heeling like a champion.

"Jeanie's a high roller. She dropped lots of names. I wouldn't have known who most of them were without her informing me." I continued to muse. "I don't know, except for you, why she showed any interest in me."

We walked on. It was getting still colder. "I wish I'd worn a coat," I remarked, trying not to shiver. I quickened my pace. Baltho kept up, still looking regal. And extremely well-trained.

I was thinking about Jeanie's loft above the shop. She told me the space was totally open. "I had a hot tub with shower built into the middle of the room," she'd said. "My oversized bed with privacy canopy is built into the floor." A bolt of lightning hit. "Wait!" I stopped dead in my tracks.

Baltho stopped. He stared up at me, as if I'd finally got his point.

"You were trying to see that we wouldn't go back and get involved, weren't you, you sly old fox," I said, patting him affectionately on the head.

"However," I added, walking on, "you and Shehera might only have been having a good time."

The Violent Still Bear It Away

"It's Christmas—we brought you a little present," my sister Diane announced from my doorstep. She walked into the house with a cat carrier in hand. She was wearing a hot-pink top with a big bottom ruffle over white stretch-pants. She was forty years old, but every time I saw her, she appeared more and more like a girl retreating to her teens.

My mom followed her in. She was in her early seventies. She looked exhausted. "My aching back," she complained, rubbing her upper buttocks. "Tom, you'll have to get my suitcase from the car."

"I'll be going home in an hour," Diane said. "It's a long drive. I want to get there before dark."

"And I'll stay with you for a few days," Mother said. "Vickie, Tim, and the kids are also in Denver. They're shopping and taking a short vacation. They'll pick me up on their way home."

Shortly after having the house where we'd grown up remodeled and expanded, Mother moved into the smaller and outdated house next door. She let Diane have her home. "She had to get away," Vickie'd told me.

"We've brought you Figaro, Figgy, for short," Diane began. She sat the carrier down in the middle of the living room.

Baltho never took his eyes off the carrier and what it held. He stood right beside it, not moving an inch.

"He's one of our favorite cats," Diane said. "See how cute the little man is." He was black with white front paws, white legs and back paws, with more white on his lower face. He had a miniature black goatee. "He's six." He was friendly, calm, and mature. I remembered him from my visits.

"I told her to bring you Figaro instead of some younger cat," Mother said. "They're more easily scared by a monster of a dog."

People had told me that I could never have a cat as long as I had Baltho. "He'd kill it," they assured me. I didn't believe them. I knew my dog. "He's no cat killer. A cat chaser, if he can get them going, but no killer," I'd answered.

Diane bent down to open the carrier. "Come on out, little boy," she cooed. "We're right here to see that nothing bad happens. Come on, baby. And Baltho, you behave yourself." She snapped her fingers to get Figgy to come out.

As if on cue, Figgy walked right out onto the living room carpet.

Just as soon as he did, Baltho started growling. He let out a deep, ferocious bark that hurt my ears. He lunged.

Instead of running, Figaro dropped to the carpet onto his side. He turned over on his back, raising his limp legs into the air to expose his belly. He purred loudly.

"Figgy is saying, 'Come hither, big boy,'" said Diane. All but Baltho remained calm.

Baltho stuck his nose into Figgy's fur, poking with some vigor and sniffing loudly, nosing him to see just what was lying there, so vulnerable, so open to inspection. I'd seen him do it to a dead squirrel and a raccoon found on our walks. Baltho, I figured, hoped he could get them to rise and run.

"Smart cat," I remarked. "You know how to show this big noise box that you have no fear."

I sat on the floor and began to stroke Figgy's tummy. Figgy purred louder and stretched.

Baltho sat down parallel to Figgy. He slid his front legs down, followed by his belly. Without a sound, he rested his head on Figgy's abdomen, as if it were a pillow.

"Trapped," I laughed.

My mom and Diane remarked in unison, "Some cat killer you are, Balthazar."

"A real brute," I added.

Mother shook her head and chuckled.

Diane soon announced, "I have to get home to take care of the kids."

"She has to get back to the menagerie," my mom said. Diane had never married and had no children. "She's got a dozen sick cats—including a pregnant mother cat that somebody just dropped off." The word was out that, under the cover of night, people could abandon unwanted cats at her house because Diane and my mom would take care of them.

"Mama Cat might have her kids any time," Diane said. "I need to be around to make sure one of the dogs or tomcats doesn't kill them." Diane bent to kiss Figgy and Baltho goodbye on their foreheads. "Be good," she said, and, with that, she left.

"Well Mother, are you hungry?" I asked. I looked at my watch. It was four-thirty. Mother liked to eat early.

"I'll be ready for dinner before long," she said.

"We'd better get started then." I motioned her to the kitchen. From the refrigerator, I took a whole chicken, rinsed it with water, split it down the middle, and laid it belly down on a Pyrex baking dish. I seasoned it with salt, pepper, and celery seeds, and stuck it in the oven. Then I placed potatoes in their jackets, and a casserole dish of scalloped corn on the same rack. Mother put together a spinach salad, with homemade vinaigrette dressing that I kept in the refrigerator.

"Dang, I forgot to buy mushrooms for this special occasion!" I exclaimed, slapping my forehead.

"You're always so thoughtful," she added, sarcastically. "You know how much I love those slimy things."

"That's why I was going to buy a couple pounds of them," I said, smiling straight at her. "We could slice some into the scalloped corn and stuff the chicken with them—all in your honor."

"Don't forget the salad," Mother said. "I love nothing more than mushrooms in my lettuce. Then, instead of enjoying it, I get to wonder where the slugs are."

"That doesn't make sense. Slugs don't hang out on mushrooms."

"Mushrooms remind me of slugs," she said.

I shrugged. "It isn't worth the energy to try to sort out your weird associations, although I'm sure they mean something."

"You *would* think so."

After dinner, I scraped the plates into Baltho's bowl of dry dog food sitting on the counter. I added some bits of the chicken neck and giblets, just as he expected. By now, he didn't get any skin. I kept his food bowl on the counter till we'd finished in the kitchen. He could eat at that time. I didn't want my mom to fall over him as he sprawled on the floor to eat. He was too tall to stand.

Mother stood at the sink to scrape and rinse dirty dishes. She handed them to me so I could load them into the dishwasher.

Out of the corner of my eye, I noticed that Baltho was standing ever-so-quietly behind her. He put his nose at the hem her skirt and inched it upwards, slightly, as if playing a child's game.

"Baltho, stop that!" Mother cried. She reached around to push Baltho's nose away. Then she pushed her skirt down.

I was busy with the dishwasher.

"Baltho!" my mom yelled again, her voice harsher than before. He was at it again. Her skirt was raised a couple of inches. "Your nose is cold!"

"Elevator going up. Nope—going down," I joked. I decided to distract him. I put his bowl on the floor in the corner. However, he was more interested in my mom. This time, she slapped his nose. "Stop it now!" she ordered. "Go eat your dinner!"

I called him over to his food. I had to put more sternness into my voice. "Get over here." He scarfed every morsel down, as if he'd never eaten.

My mom had only heard about his antics on the phone. She'd not yet experienced them firsthand. "You've got your hands full with him," she said.

"He's probably telling us something important," I said.

"That he's too darned playful. That's what he's saying," she said. I knew her—she'd supply the reading she favored.

"I dunno. We'll have to think about it." I placed my finger under my chin. I was ready to give her a hard time. I knew from various phone conversations and letters that soon she'd start in on me for not being a Biblical literalist. According to her pastor, everyone who failed to accept every single word of the Old and New Testaments as literally true was not a Christian. The Bible needed no interpretation, no taking the history and sociology of the times into account. Never mind that such a system threw the believer into various contradictions and absurdities, as

St. Augustine long ago pointed out in his many works on Biblical interpretation.

My mother would usually come to her senses in the end, but moving her in the right direction could present serious problems. Her first reactions tended to be prickly. I would have to persist.

Intuiting what was coming, I suggested we move to the living room and sit in front of the window. The winged-back rocking chairs were calming. I suspected she'd go further than carping that I wasn't literalist and express her disdain for my so-called liberal social and religious views. Her pastor was up in arms against the so-called liberal agenda threatening America.

She sat on the chair and began rocking, slowly, definitely. "What will people think of you?" she asked.

I knew what she alluding to but was rather taken aback by her question. "Do you really think many contemporary people will condemn me for not being a Christian according to your pastor's narrow definition?" I asked. I sat on the chair across from her. "I'm far more educated than he is," I added.

"Being more educated doesn't make you right," she said.

"It may not make me right, but it certainly makes me more aware of the complexities and pitfalls of interpretation," I said, feeling the urge to get sarcastic. Baltho sat quietly between us. He didn't stretch himself upward so that we couldn't see each other's faces. He sat like a good dog, one that doesn't demand too much attention.

"You've gone so far left in your thinking," she said.

"Have I?" I rocked. "Mother, you're losing all sense of direction there in the provinces under the tutelage of a bumpkin who believes he knows everything. Clearly, you've now got someone else trying to run the family system. You're prone to that, you know." I paused, trying to keep my rocking steady and slow, instead of speeding up with aggression. "Mother, you really need to find another pastor, one who's enlightened both by scholarship and maturity."

Figaro had adopted a place at the end of the couch and was fast asleep. My mom got up to get the blanket from the other end of the couch. She opened it, wrapped the warmth around herself, and sat down in the rocking chair again. "Your house is always so cold."

"I wear a sweater in the winter, so I don't waste heat. In many ways, I'm truly conservative," I said. I wanted to make sure she was better schooled in the meanings behind those liberal versus conservative labels that she was being encouraged to brandish like daggers.

"My son," she began, "chairs panels for PFLAG, Parents and Friends of Lesbians and Gays—an organization whose purpose is to advance the gay agenda." She shivered.

This seemed the root of her fear—my support of gays and lesbians. "Armed with such facts, you'll soon accuse me of advancing the pro-abortion agenda, when you know my opinion is that abortion should be a private matter between a woman, her medical, psychological, and spiritual counsel—and, I'd hope, the man involved," I said. I looked over at Baltho. "Never mind. I know you're repeating the simplistic slogans your pastor throws around. PFLAG tries to educate people about sexual orientation and stop the rampant abuse of people who are not fully straight." I reached out to pet Baltho's head and shoulders. "Mother, you'd never advocate the mistreatment of African Americans or Hispanics, would you?"

She sat up tall. "Of course not."

"I knew you weren't a bigot at heart. This is no different. Both PFLAG panels I've chaired have been held in a United Methodist church. One that I almost chaired was held in a United Church of Christ sanctuary, or was it Lutheran?"

"Liberal churches," Mother retorted.

"Oh, that's right—mainline denominations aren't really Christian."

Baltho turned to look directly at my mother. I could imagine his wondering, "Where are you from, Mrs.—another dimension that parallels our own, but only in certain ways?"

"Mother, do you remember that I was also a campus chaplain—and my primary area of scholarly expertise is the great Christian writers of the seventeenth century—Donne, Herbert, Milton? Many were pastors. All were highly educated men, who worked hard to mature in the faith. And help others grow in grace and wisdom."

She became as rigid as a stone.

I began again. "This wedge being driven between conservatives and liberals makes no sense."

She made no sound.

"I believe in conserving the best of the past, in understanding and valuing our heritage—and in not being wasteful about resources, fiscal and tangible ones that affect the planet. You know that," I said. I hoped what I said would sink in. "But in other ways, I'm liberal. Liberal means free, generous, and open to new ideas. But overall, I'm a moderate. I try to avoid extremes."

"That isn't how those terms are used now," she replied, her hands still in her lap.

"I don't care what those who prefer simplistic slogans to true reflection say. We must think about complex issues in ways that do them justice." Baltho shifted his weight, as if listening carefully. "I'll remind you of the sexual spectrum. Hardly anyone is fully gay or fully straight. So much depends on the circumstances of one's life, and one's experiences. Genes play a part in the mix as well. A large part."

I had explained this to family members before, but evidently the concept was too complex for my mom, especially with a pastor who kept pushing her, and the church—rather, *his* church—further and further to the right.

"As the oldest child, I was reared to help solve the problems of our very dysfunctional family, as you know. You don't really expect me to stop trying, do you?" I asked.

Mother said nothing, but raised her face to the ceiling, adopting the pose of a martyr.

A light went on in my mind. "When Baltho helps with therapy, he typically homes in on the central problem," I said, thinking aloud. I paused. "Over the years, we've been moving toward this point. There's no better time to get further into the sexual problems that have long afflicted our family."

She groaned.

Baltho groaned with her—only he was louder.

I couldn't help but laugh. "Like your best friend Cynthia, you had a miserable marriage to a violent man," I said.

"Cynthia likes to be the dominant partner in relationships."

"In less obvious ways, you also fought for dominance in your marriage." From my mom's facial expression, and the way her body drew back, I could tell she didn't want to hear more. "It was really your mom channeled through you who wanted to control the entire system. *Through* you, is key."

"My mother was a good mother. She worried about everyone."

"I know she tried to be good, and had lots of good traits," I said. "But her constant worry—and interference—was an expression of control." I paused again to check my mom's response. "I always hope if I keep repeating core concepts that you'll understand them—kind of like St. Paul on the road to Damascus. When he met the risen Christ, the scales dropped from his eyes. He realized that his false beliefs had been making him persecute Christ all along."

Baltho raised his head up between my mother and me so that we had to take notice. His gesture seemed to be some kind of visual punctuation, calling attention to the truth of what I'd just said.

Mother didn't say a word, but she looked stung. Her hands were knotted in her lap. She had a way of making me feel mean for pressing her. She used to tell me I was killing her when I said anything negative to her. Because of my own personal work, including therapy, I would now remind her that she was stronger than that.

"You're killing me. I feel like I can't breathe," she said.

"True criticism never hurt anyone," I reminded her. "We can't grow without it."

"It makes me feel like you're sitting on my chest and choking me," she responded.

"No one likes criticism." I paused. "Your emotional reaction is pretty violent. You know that, don't you?"

Baltho nudged over to be closer to her, as if to comfort her, now that she was starting to open up. He whimpered a little, as if to sympathize. "I'm hoping those scales will fully and finally drop from your eyes," I said. "So is Baltho."

I saw no outward signs of that happening. Her posture remained rigid.

"I think Baltho was playing elevator skirt because he wants you to own your sexuality so that you can allow others to own theirs. He's never done that to anyone else. You've always been repressed."

She smiled slightly. Baltho put his head down on her lap and sighed. He acted as he did with Carmen.

My mom didn't move her hands, as I'd hoped she'd do. She continued to ignore him, even though he whimpered a little, coaxing her to pet him. She wanted to ignore me too. Baltho pressed his head into her lap. His whimpering became more insistent. He demanded that Mother comfort him.

"Persecuting others in the name of God is wrong, especially when you go after those who already suffer rejection, maiming, even murder."

She started to raise her hand slightly.

I thought she was going to swat Baltho. My muscles tensed. I was ready to rescue him.

But, to my relief, her hands loosened from the knot in her lap. "Oh Baltho," she said, "you really are a big, big pest." She began to pet him. "I still say you have to be careful. I'd hate to see you on the news, arrested in some sort of sex scandal."

"Why would I be arrested in a sex scandal?" I asked, wanting to lash her for even harboring such a bizarre notion. "Knowing yourself doesn't mean you act on every temptation. In fact, you're less likely to act out if you confront and own your Shadow—that is, what you don't want others to see."

"So you say."

"I'll remind you of the former Dean of the Cathedral," I said. She knew something of my many confrontations with him when I was a university campus chaplain in the 80s— but not the depth or frequency. "He always hinted at things, as if letting the curtain lift for a moment. But he never really revealed anything about himself. The media took care of that by exposing his arrest. He could no longer keep his Shadow secret."

Mother knew I no longer wanted to be in formal ministry as a result of my experiences at the Cathedral. "People operate from the Shadow Side when they fail to acknowledge their issues. To own your issues, you have to face them and explore what you need to explore. Then you find a true sense of self." I paused, hoping the truth would sink in.

Mother seemed to be developing a mother-child bond with Baltho. Based on her tender petting of his head and shoulders, I hoped she might be able to carry that genuine concern over to her son.

"I know you worry so much about sex scandals because of your family history." I laughed a little nervously. This was a subject my mom never wanted to think about. When I was still a toddler, two male relatives, one a minor and one middle-aged, got caught in a gay sex ring that involved several prominent townsmen.

"Mother, I don't for one minute believe that my dad's family was without their own sexual issues," I said. "I know what happened to him. So do you."

"You know he was off his rocker when that happened," Mother answered. "He wasn't gay."

"All my life he raged about 'all the queers' in your family. His hyper-masculine posturing gave him a good excuse to abuse everyone who got in his way, especially those he perceived as weak—like women. That's the trouble with men who don't grasp their own sexuality. They have to prove their dominance over everyone and everything."

Mother said nothing, her hand moving slowly along Baltho's head and neck.

"I would remind you of Micah 6:8: 'He hath shewed thee, O man, what is good; and what doth the LORD require of thee, but to do justly, and to love mercy, and to walk humbly with thy God?'"

Mother kept petting Baltho, her hand movements methodical, neither speeding up nor slowing down. I kept my rocking just as even. Perhaps she was listening this time. Bible verses used well seemed essential to her healing. Whenever I went to my hometown to see my family, the many out-of-control animals as well as Diane did little but distract, keeping all serious discussions at bay. That's why I'd refused to return to my hometown for a few years. I wasn't going to get sucked back into the dysfunctional family system typified by erratic attempts to grope at balanced and, thus, real relationships.

"Such issues are normal in American families," I added. "Problems with sex and religion abound. That's what those PFLAG panels I chaired were about. Americans can't seem to find a balance."

I let my words sink in. Then I reminded Mother of one of her dad's prominent forebears, Jacques LaRamee. "Remember his legacy," I said. "He was well known as an explorer and fur-trapper in the upper Rockies. He was just, honest, and treated others—including the often-despised native Americans—well." I paused, so Mother could meditate on a better aspect of her family history.

She was listening. She liked hearing about forebears of good repute.

"Jacques shared with fellow free-trappers his theory that the world was wide and there was room enough for all. He had the courage to live his convictions. He didn't follow what was imposed on him from the outside."

"Your grandfather liked to talk about him," Mother said, remembering.

I nodded. "Jacques had compassion for starving Indians when others didn't. When he later became a rancher, he let them kill and eat one of his cattle. Because he wasn't worried about his masculinity, he could be strong in good ways."

Baltho whimpered, as if to suggest that my mom needed to give him more attention. She began to pet him with both hands.

"Women who own their masculinity, along with their femininity, are much happier. They have better relationships too." I noticed a pained look on her face. "You shot me out into this world of pain and suffering, so I figure I have the right to push back," I laughed.

"When you feel like it, you never hesitate to sting like a wasp."

I laughed again. "Think of the pain as birth pangs. You needed to have a son who reminded you to take hold of your Shadow and bring it back inside yourself, where it belongs—part of your whole being—not projected onto others."

Mother petted Baltho's head thoughtfully. "I wonder what happened in my family?" she asked. "How did they forget Jacques' message?"

"Victorianism set in," I said. "Jacques left the appearance of civilization to explore the greater reality. In the wild, he tested his own nature and found a genuine sense of self."

Mother didn't object.

"The family should have emphasized that aspect of its heritage over the upholders of the status quo—those who reject what they deem *not them*. Victorians often show us that what they choose to condemn, and ignore, is indeed *them*—written in italics."

Mother's face had finally relaxed. At last, she'd seemed to reach a place of understanding. I didn't know how much we could build on that understanding during her stay—I didn't even know how long she'd be around.

Figgy came over and looked up at her. Baltho moved his head over, so that Figgy could jump up on her lap and lie down.

"See, the family can come together and enjoy each other's company, once we've faced up to things with an open heart and mind," I said. I hoped her journey to a real self might continue, even after she returned to the narrow-mindedness of our hometown. But then, I'd been hoping so for a long time.

Letting It Out

My former client Carmen had told Manuel that I could work wonders. He was about the same age as she, in his late twenties. When I opened my front door, he stood on my doorstep, but faced backwards. He looked out on my neighborhood.

"It's cold today," I said, bidding him in.

"Carmen said I'd be reminded of my home in Honduras." He nodded, approvingly. "We don't have winter there." He turned to face me, pulling his winter coat close, and shivered. "I'm glad we don't have snow on the ground. It makes taking the bus harder."

"So far, January hasn't been bad," I said.

"Carmen told me you don't have the attitude of a Gringo. She said your dog is like a great, dark wolf. He knows just what you need."

"Still going by her kiddy book illustrations," I said, laughing. "At least Baltho's a good wolf. He also acts like her child."

"She told me."

"That would make her Mama Wolf," I said, laughing.

The ice was broken. Manuel laughed and stepped inside, to be greeted in the foyer by both Baltho and his cat Figaro standing side by side. Baltho pushed his head into Manuel's hand, and Figgy stood on his back legs and reached his paws up to stroke Manuel's pant leg. He did not extend his claws. "She didn't tell me about a cat," Manuel exclaimed.

"Figgy is a new addition," I said.

With a hand on both animals, Manuel remarked, "It's good to have two hands." Both Baltho and Figgy stretched and preened for him. "I especially like cats. They are quiet and don't get in the way. They seem very normal."

"Well this cat thinks he's a dog, and Mr. Dog, also known as Baltho, likes that. I don't know that most people would consider it very normal," I joked, motioning for Manuel to sit in one of the winged-back rocking chairs in front of the window. "But we don't care. We like unusual things in our home—just as long as they're friendly."

"My grandparents raised me. We had no electricity and meager food. They told me I had to be normal."

I nodded. "Your English is remarkably good."

"I have studied for many years," Manuel said. "I wanted to be normal and get a good job."

I noted Manuel's frequent use of the word normal.

"When I was little, my grandparents often kept me in a pen with the pigs and chickens outside. I couldn't run away. I tried to do nothing to upset them, or I would never be let me out."

He was given the opportunity to study English offered by missionaries in Honduras. "Soon, I met my future wife. She was my teacher, an American girl. She was only a little older than me. We moved to Colorado and had a baby." He paused, looking distressed. He appeared to have difficulty proceeding. "A few years later, my wife wanted a divorce, and I lost my job. It wasn't much anyway, but it was a job."

"How long have you been out of work?" I asked.

"Many months," he replied. "I'm no longer looking. I have given up." He paused again, petting Figgy, who had jumped up on his lap. "My social worker finally permitted me to see you," he said. "Social Services will pay you. They want me to be productive." Baltho sat quietly at his side, offering his support too.

Manuel was especially gracious, bright, although lacking in formal education. In Honduras, he joined his wife's church, some sort of strict Pentecostal sect. He'd gained United States citizenship. Recently, he'd become a Hare Krishna. "We spend most of our time fasting, singing, and praying. I eat no meat. I am a strict vegetarian," he said. He lived in community with others in a house they owned on Eighth Avenue in East Denver.

"Do you have visitation rights?" I asked.

"Yes, I have them, but my wife allows me to visit my son only as she wishes," Manuel related. "I am supposed to be able to have Charlie every other week. She will not let him stay with me and the Hare Krishnas. They would welcome him."

"Do you demand your rights?" I asked.

Manuel shook his head. He stared at the carpet, as if all fight had been stolen from him. He didn't feel comfortable with the system. "I do not demand anything."

"That doesn't upset you?" I asked.

"Yes," he answered. "But I do not know what to do. I am not normal."

I asked about his work history.

"I have washed dishes. I had a part-time janitorial job, and I have made hamburgers at McDonalds. That's the last job I had." He sounded as though he'd gone through this list many times before. "It wasn't that I've ever demanded much. I would have been okay cleaning floors at McDonalds. But they didn't want me even doing that. They thought I wasn't normal."

"Did they use that word?" I asked.

"No, they said I didn't fit in," Manuel replied. Baltho placed his head in Manuel's lap and sighed. "I knew what they meant. They meant I wasn't normal. It has been the same problem all my life."

"You're very thin," I observed. "You said you're a strict vegetarian. I wonder if you eat enough."

"I have terrible stomach aches," Manuel responded. "Most of the time, my stomach hurts too much to eat. But I eat fruits, vegetables, whole grains, and, sometimes, I sneak a little fish, when I can afford it. We aren't supposed to, but sometimes we get very hungry, and vegetarian food alone does not satisfy."

"Have you seen a doctor about your stomach problems?" I asked.

Manuel nodded. He'd seen several doctors. "My wife wanted to have me committed," he volunteered, seemingly out of nowhere.

"Mine tried that tack too," I recalled. "What was your wife's reason?" I asked.

"She wanted to get rid of me."

I smiled a cynical smile. "Also sounds familiar."

"She made me see doctors," Manuel said.

"What did the doctors say?"

"They said I was sane. I have poor self-esteem. I don't have a strong sense of self. But nobody has really helped me. I prefer natural methods of healing. I'm afraid of prescription medicine and medical doctors."

Manuel was very forthcoming, as many who have had lots of therapy are. For two weeks I listened to the details of his life. During Manuel's third session, Baltho stood right in front of him, putting his nose near his. Manuel and Baltho were about the same height. Baltho burped loudly, and then burped again, repeating the sequence. Then he farted. Not once, not twice, but three times.

"Baltho, what did you eat?" I demanded. Baltho came to me.

"Don't be ashamed of your dog," Manuel said. Figgy jumped off his lap. Manuel's voice was comforting. "Your face got red right after the second burp."

"I don't know what's gotten into him," I replied. I reached out to pet him. "He's my dog, no matter what. He knows that."

"Is his behavior normal?" Manuel asked, thoughtfully.

"Well if you have to burp, you have to burp. What surprised me is that he got right in your face to do it. He's never done that to anyone else."

"Is it normal to get embarrassed for your dog?" Manuel asked.

I pondered Manuel's question. "Well, I don't know if it's a good thing. But I was embarrassed over his bad behavior. That, I would say, is pretty normal, for someone who cares about his dog and his clients." I shifted my position. "Manuel, this dog often shows me important truths that I've missed," I said. My mind had begun to connect the dots. "Do you by any chance have lots of gas? You've never said anything about flatulence, but I'm wondering."

"Oh yes," Manuel said, as if relieved to admit it. "I have gas all the time." As I had come to expect, Manuel asked, "Is that normal?"

"I guess that depends on your constitution and diet. Most things seem a combination of genes and environment," I said. "You eat lots of fiber, right?"

Manuel nodded.

Baltho nodded. He had gone to stand in front of Manuel again. I wondered if he was going to burp or fart again.

"Do you eat lots of onions and broccoli, cabbage and beans, things that give most of us gas?" I asked.

Baltho, the Dog Who Owned a Man

Manuel nodded.

The picture was becoming clearer. "Do you do anything about the gas such foods make in normal people?"

Manuel looked puzzled, as if he didn't understand my question.

"There are natural products like Beano that are supposed to keep gas from building up. You might try that."

"I have. They don't seem to help."

"Do you burp or fart? Do you release the gas?" I asked. "Baltho seems to have been showing us a solution. Or part of one."

"Oh no," Manuel said. "I was always told that expelling gas is not normal." He paused. He looked down at his lap in shame. "Is it?" he asked, rather sheepishly. "Is it not abnormal?"

I said nothing, letting Manuel think more about the normal-abnormal axis on which so much of his world turned.

"My grandparents said good children didn't make such noises and offend everyone by their smells. They put me in the cage when I did so."

Instead of saying that Manuel's grandparents seemed extreme, I said, "Well, it's true that it isn't considered polite to burp or fart in public, though boys and men sometimes think it's funny."

"They do?" Manuel asked, his eyebrows screwing up into question marks. He shook his head, lowered his eyes, and clucked disapprovingly, as I imagined his grandparents might have done.

"I think Baltho is showing us that you should burp or fart—or both—if you need to. You'll feel better if you get rid of the gas. Excuse yourself if you're with people and go outside—or to the bathroom. Somewhere by yourself.

While it isn't considered polite in good company, it certainly is normal to need to get rid of gas. No wonder your stomach aches."

When Baltho, Figgy, and I greeted Manuel at the door the following weeks, his smile grew bigger each time. "Every day, I feel better, just like this spring weather in winter," he exclaimed. He looked up at the clear, sunlit sky, then at me and the animals. "I have only to take digestives now and then. I no longer feel the terrible pains that felt like I needed to have a baby." He stepped inside.

I laughed, deep and heartily. "Where did you come up with that colorful notion?" I asked.

"My grandmother. When I had a stomach ache, she'd ask if it was bad enough to have a baby. If it wasn't, she told me to be quiet."

"And act normal," I said.

Manuel nodded. He laughed.

"That you can laugh about it also shows progress," I said. "I want you to realize that."

Baltho, sitting between us, burped once, loudly.

Manuel burped back, loud and long.

I winced, wondering what might come next. "Perhaps I ought to step out of the room till the air clears," I remarked. I was glad the weather was warm enough to open the front door and a window. I laughed as I let in some air.

"Carmen was right. This dog is very smart," Manuel said. He paused to think. "And very normal. So is the cat."

"I see you're firmly on the road to healing. Now that you're stronger, I want you to concentrate on getting a job"

Manuel was coming to realize what everyone needs to know. Normalcy depends on the eye of the beholder and isn't therefore a good indicator of one's worth. "You're becoming stronger all the time. Strong enough to take a stand and assert yourself. Only you can decide what's important to you."

"Strong enough to kick some ass," he said, his mouth forming a big grin.

I laughed. "I've never seen you so bold. Whose ass do you plan to start on?"

He shrugged and laughed. "I was just acting normal. That's how men talk."

"Maybe you'll want to assert your parental rights and see your son more often."

"Yes," Manuel said without hesitation.

Specters

It was a crisp and sunny Sunday morning in mid-March. Manuel phoned to say he'd been hired by a small local company that packaged herbs for the local grocery stores. "They like me. I work with four others, two men and two women. I am happy," he answered. He didn't expect a big job since he didn't have much education. "They say I can move up to delivery if I work hard. I will."

The bells of Mount Carmel, Our Lady of Guadalupe, and St. Patrick's began ringing. They created a cacophony from many directions that blended into harmony and then back into cacophony again. March had come in like a lamb and remained like one—frisky and energizing.

On our walk later that day, Baltho and I passed a group of boys playing in one of the front yards. Although Figgy usually wanted to walk with us, I was afraid he'd get hit by a car or eaten by one of the rampaging dogs because he didn't stay close but investigated interesting smells as Baltho and I moved forward. So he had to stay home, safe inside. These weren't boys we knew—we were several blocks from home but not on one of our usual routes.

One little boy of perhaps four years old, wearing a black cape, ran up to me, taking my forearm. The others reached out to pet Baltho. "Mister, I want to suck, to suck—"

I pulled back a little, my muscles tensing. I almost asked, "What in the world have these older boys had been teaching you?" The therapist in me envisioned a lifetime of therapy stretching out over a long, rocky road for this abused child.

One of the bigger boys bent down, looked the little one in the eye, and said, "I want to suck your blood! That's how you say it. You have to say all of it, not just part."

I laughed. Boy, was I glad I didn't say anything. When I looked more closely, I realized the youngest boy was also wearing a set of fangs. He struggled to keep them in his mouth. They weren't helping him say things correctly.

"Could I suck Baltho's blood?" the little boy asked. His eyes were big and his gaze hypnotic.

"You know his name?" I asked.

"Baltho's a macho dog. He beat up Tiny. Everybody knows about that."

I laughed. "We have to get back to our house," I explained. "I need to do some gardening that I didn't do first thing this morning. Besides, Baltho needs to keep his blood."

"Could you send Baltho over to play with us later?" one of the older boys asked.

I saw that the little boy was moving his face closer to Baltho's neck. "You're so hungry," I remarked. I couldn't help but laugh. "Maybe you could pretend to suck a little of Baltho's blood. Baltho loves attention, and that would make you happy, wouldn't it?"

The boy nodded and smiled, his fangs almost falling out again.

"But just pretend," I instructed, watching the boy put his mouth on Baltho's neck. "Don't bite." Baltho had just been groomed, but I still hoped the boy wouldn't get sick from any germs on Baltho's hair. Baltho put his nose up to the child's ear and nuzzled him. The boy began to laugh. "He's kissing me." Baltho's tongue darted out a little and then returned to his mouth. Those were indeed Baltho kisses. He never slurped.

"I think that's enough, don't you," I remarked. I slowly began to inch away, knowing that Baltho would follow. "We'll have to talk to you later," I said.

"We'll have to talk to you later," the boys repeated. "We won't forget!" the boys called after us. "You and Baltho are doing a good job. Your gardens are really beautiful," they said.

I smiled. I wondered if these were some of the kids that Mrs. Sardini told me she'd had to chase off at various times because they were jumping over the fence to pick our flowers. Baltho kept looking back, as if he wanted to go back and play with the boys. "We need to get home," I told him, coaxing him on.

Before turning the corner to our house, Baltho and I passed the house of one of our older neighbors. Mr. Contini had probably been born in that house, just as some of the other Italian neighbors had. Every year, he added at least two new statues to his yard. Mr. Contini was fond of painting them in the classical manner. He didn't lay on the bright yellows, blues, and reds of his ancient Italian ancestors. Strangely, his Venus de Milo had always remained plain white cement. But he painted the flesh of all the others a nice fawn color and highlighted their lips with a dark, brownish-red. He never neglected to paint a few beauty marks on their cheeks or chins—even on the statues of boys with donkeys and carts, which he seemed especially fond of.

Around the perimeter of his lot stood dozens of neatly-trimmed roses of all hues, like sentries guarding his property. His one-hundred-foot tall catalpa tree at the back of the yard put on quite a show every spring. Panicles of white, bell-shaped flowers with orange and purple spots and stripes would open, and soon fall, spreading over the ground like a late, spring snow.

That day, Mr. Contini stood outside. This was the first time I'd seen him since I moved back. Walking slowly along the perimeter of his yard, he looked down at his roses, inspecting each one. I'd many times watched him carry out this routine when I'd lived in my townhome in the 1980s. I did it in the common area gardens myself.

Usually, Mr. Contini would see me, and we'd at least tip our heads back in acknowledgment of each another. But this morning, he didn't look at me. Surely he saw me. I noticed that Baltho's eyes also followed Mr. Contini's movements around the perimeter of his yard. Mr. Contini looked past Baltho too.

Baltho and I strode onwards. If I hadn't needed to get back to the house and leave for several appointments at my Cherry Creek office, I would have crossed the street to speak with him. I wondered how he and his family were.

A few days later, when Baltho and I walked past the Continis' home, I saw his daughter and his wife standing in the yard. With age, the women had grown to look more alike. Both wore dark stockings rolled down just below their knees and held by garters. Old Mrs. Contini however, appeared more bent and walked haltingly. Her face was ashen and heavily lined. Because her English wasn't good, I never knew whether she really understood me.

"Let's go talk with the Continis," I said to Baltho. We crossed the street to greet them. The daughter wasn't a big talker, but her English was pretty good. She would fill me in.

"I saw your dad the other morning when Baltho and I walked by, but he didn't speak," I began. "I didn't have time, or I would have crossed the street to say hello. How is everyone?"

The daughter said something to her mother in Italian. She and her mother looked at me in consternation. Then they glanced at each other.

"Your dad never said much, but the other day he seemed too preoccupied with his roses to really see me. It was as if I wasn't there."

The daughter said something to her mother again. I figured she was translating what I'd said to her. Mrs. Contini looked even more puzzled and shrugged.

"He's all right, isn't he?" I asked, more than a little concerned about their reaction.

Finally the daughter said, "My father is dead. He died last summer."

"When?" I asked.

"On Pentecost," she answered.

"I'm sorry. I didn't know. I was gone for awhile."

"That's all right," the daughter said.

"Does he have a brother or relative who looks like him?" I asked. "I swear I saw him just the other day."

"No, no one," the mother said. Her comprehension of English seemed much better than I had previously realized.

"I saw him," I explained. "He was standing outside, looking over the yard, walking along the perimeter, examining his roses, just as he always did. My dog Baltho tracked his movements along with me."

"You must have seen his ghost," the daughter said. She explained that she'd moved back into the house after he'd died so she could take care of her mother.

"That must have been the case," I said, explaining that I sometimes did have such experiences. "In the Apostles Creed, we say we believe in the Communion of Saints, in the communion of both the living and dead. I believe your dad would still be concerned about his yard and his family, even though he's passed on."

Talking about my personal beliefs involving the souls of the departed and their visitations always made me a little nervous. Although my frame of reference was Christian, I hoped that people could see similar patterns across many religious and spiritual systems.

I realized fleetingly that I had more paranormal experiences than I often remembered. They were woven so tightly into the fabric of my life that I usually gave them little thought.

Sometimes I was shown things people hadn't divulged. Not necessarily bad things. When something was revealed, I knew what was, or what would be—no matter how much people denied, blamed me, or tried to deflect the truth.

I wondered if these old-fashioned Italians—Catholic, I was certain—would make the sign of the cross and ask me to leave.

"Yes," old Mrs. Contini nodded in halting English. "He would look at his yard," she said, as if her mind were active. "He wouldn't like all the weeds we let pass."

I laughed. "Your yard isn't weedy. But it isn't as manicured as it used to be when Mr. Contini was alive and caring for it every day."

"We have not put in any new statues," the daughter added, looking wilted. She glanced around as if she too were concerned about the messiness of the place and their failure to keep things exactly as Mr. Contini would have wished. "We have been very sad," the daughter said, her mother nodding in agreement.

Baltho sat, as if making known his understanding that we would be awhile. I wondered what else he was thinking. "We know we should be taking better care," said the daughter. "We've let things fall apart."

"I'm sure your dad understands. When people die, everyone goes through a transition. Your dad has probably been going through changes too. Everyone has to adjust to a new state of being."

The daughter related a funny story. "Papa's doctor said he had to get more exercise—more than working in his yard every day," she said. "So he walked three blocks." She began to perambulate the grounds, slowly, like her aged father. "He walked down to Patsy's Bar and drank a glass of red wine or two, *Italiano solamente*. Then, he walked back home." She wobbled slowly back to me and her mother.

I laughed. "Lots of exercise, right."

Mrs. Contini tilted her head back. "Yes," she said—and laughed.

Baltho stood up. He looked happy, as if we'd accomplished what needed to be done. "We can go now," I said.

"I believe it's good to talk with our deceased relatives and friends when we feel the need. It helps us move through our grief and embrace life again. Certainly talking to them won't hurt them either."

The Continis nodded. "Yes," they said. "We will talk." Their faces looked relieved, their postures straightened.

Most of my experiences with the souls of the dead had been auditory. This one was visual. I wondered why. Perhaps my experience with Mr. Contini was to help his family move on. They needed to realize that he wasn't coming back to haunt them and make them feel guilty about all that they'd neglected to do—but rather to see how his gardens, his wife, and his daughter were doing. If we have cared about one another in life, surely we continue to care about one another even after our bodies have died.

Talk About It

The phone was ringing, loud, insistent. I tried to ignore it, but it kept ringing. I didn't know why the answering machine downstairs didn't pick up. I opened my eyes and glanced at the clock on the nightstand. Two-thirty in the morning. The answering machine finally came on. I heard my voice, then another voice, a loud voice, with an insistent tone, leaving a message. It might be an emergency involving one of my clients.

I fumbled for the receiver on the nightstand next to me.

"This is Ramon," the voice on the other end announced. "Mark from your men's group is my boyfriend." The group had recently decided to take a break for an undetermined amount of time. Many of the men felt they'd learned a lot about themselves and taken ownership of their issues. They vowed they'd no longer shove them under the rug, where the issues could trip them—and others trying to get near.

Just before we disbanded, Mark said he'd decided to try a relationship with a man. He'd not had any success with women.

"Just remember," I said, "you probably won't find a gay relationship much different from a straight one. However, it's more difficult in this way—you're less likely to have the support of family and friends."

"I'm calling to tell you I'm shooting that son of a bitch," Ramon said, braying me out of my reverie. He sounded drunk. "I have a gun, and I'm going upstairs to shoot that asshole."

"Ramon, I want you to get calm and think about what you're saying."

"He doesn't want me! He told me to move out of his house."

"I want you to put the gun down and call 911. I'll get dressed and be right over."

"No. I'm shooting Mark now," Ramon cried.

"I'm sure you don't want to do that," I said, wishing I had someone who could use another line and call 911 for me. "You know you'd find yourself in terrible trouble. You're mad at Mark. I know you don't want to shoot him. You really do care about him, don't you?"

Ramon went silent.

"Ramon, you care about Mark. I'm sure of that," I repeated. "We don't shoot people we care about, even though we feel forced into a corner when our feelings get hurt."

"Bang!" I heard a shot. The line went dead.

I jumped out of bed and called 911. I told them to get over to Mark's house immediately. The 911 operator said, "Stay home. Do *not* go over there. You don't want to get shot."

I paced the floor for awhile. I let Baltho out into the courtyard and then let him in.

I finally went upstairs and tried to get back to sleep, with Baltho following. He jumped up on the bed with me, wrapping his foreleg around my arm. I worried, wondered if I'd hear anything soon. I hoped to God Ramon hadn't shot Mark—or himself.

Even though I tried calling Mark the next day, I could find out nothing. Two days went by. I worried intensely. I was terrified that I might get into trouble for failing my client, even though he was not actively so at the time. Our medical doctor, Betty, whom I was consulting about the issue, kept me grounded. I'd informed Gold but didn't ask for his advice.

Then a call. "Tom." Mark's voice was on the other end of the line.

I breathed with relief.

"That crazy son of a bitch shot a hole in the ceiling and ran out of the house with the gun. The cops found it in the back yard. They still haven't found him," he said.

"Where are you?" I asked.

"Staying with friends. The police told me it would be best if I didn't go home for a while, just in case he comes back."

"Do you want to set an appointment to talk?" I asked.

"I'm all right. We can talk about it when we start the group again," he said. "I'm OK. I'm just glad to be rid of him. I need some time to think."

"Okay. Just remember that you can call or see me when you're ready."

Just as soon as I got off the line with Mark, the phone rang again. "Tommy, where are you?" Gold's voice boomed from the other end. "I've got you down for 11:00, and it's 11:20. Your hour is half-gone."

Baltho came up and stood beside me. He put his head under my left hand so that I felt his presence. He wanted me to know that I had his support in standing up to Gold. "I never scheduled for 11:00," I said. "I've told you—I don't have enough clients to warrant weekly supervisions."

"You need to talk about that guy who tried to shoot your client."

"Thanks, but as you know, I've been talking with Betty about it." I hadn't asked Gold for supervision because I wanted to confer with someone who had more medical knowledge than he had. "I don't need double supervision."

"Well, Tommy, you know I'm going to have to charge you for my time," Gold said, his voice condescending.

"I told you—I didn't schedule. We've had this argument more times than I can count."

Gold felt like turning the screws. "With me you get not only outstanding supervision and teaching, but also personal psychotherapy for yourself," he trumpeted.

"You mean that ironically, don't you?" I said, hanging up.

I petted Baltho's head and hugged him to me, receiving the strength he offered.

I wondered what Gold thought he was teaching me when, on our last perambulatory supervision, involving another lunch, he went into Walgreen's to look for reading glasses. "Mine are scratched," he said. "I've sat on them too many times." Finding a pair he liked, Gold happened to leave his old ones in the self-service display and walked out with the new ones pushed back on his forehead.

I'd heard through colleagues that Gold had never been in therapy himself. I'd never asked because I didn't trust that he'd tell the truth. The more I saw of him, the more I believed the rumors.

"I dreamed the other night that I found myself in the movie *Jaws*," I told him. In the context of our confrontation, I figured he'd realize he was the shark.

"You know that's a psychosexual dream. You're being devoured by your sexuality," he said. "You really need to hook up with someone and get laid. It isn't normal to have only a dog for a companion. You need sex on a regular basis."

I harrumphed and walked away. Gold had an answer for everything, one that turned the tables on the person who dared to confront him—one that kept him from taking any responsibility.

It was no wonder my colleague Brenda told me she was staying as far away from the offices as she could and seeing her clients at home. "I can't stand the chaos that Gold creates everywhere. I've never seen such an unsettled, manipulative person," she said. "His intelligence makes him more dangerous."

After she made this change, Gold began expressing to colleagues how worried he was about Brenda. "She's becoming more and more unreliable and resistant. I hear she's back on drugs again."

"Again?" I asked. I wondered if she'd ever been on drugs. I guessed this was another Gold tactic. Others had managed to quit Gold's practice shortly after joining. They had all kinds of excuses: their husbands didn't want them spending so much time away from their families; their children needed them; they were having serious health problems. One woman said she was near a nervous breakdown. She acted like it. Gold hadn't helped.

Marty was the only therapist who'd been with the Golds for years—for over a decade, I'd heard. Marty told me Gold was lonely. "That's why he demands we stay near. He needs those regular chats, even if only by phone."

On my way down the hall to Gold's office the previous week, Emma's door stood open. She looked up from her desk. "He's changing his clothes," she said. "I had to drive home to get clean ones for him." Her set jaw showed that she was annoyed. "If my husband didn't require his daily three lunches with supervisees and clients, he might be able to keep his clothes clean." The Golds had a meeting with the mayor later that afternoon. Emma rarely said a word that could be construed as criticism of him. He'd told me what a monster his first wife was—manipulative, resistant, she even attended sex parties. Emma would stay with him until the end, he'd told me. "Just as Marty will do. So will you. I know people," he said.

When I entered Gold's office, I expressed annoyance that, as usual, he never listened. "It's always something. Today you're distracted by having to change your clothes. I don't need this," I said. "You don't give supervisions but side shows. I'm tired of being screwed."

"Well, if you hold on for a little, you can experience that too," he said.

"You can forget that."

Pondering my latest interactions with Gold, I reached down to pet Baltho as I sat down at my desk "Oh Baltho, what a mess I've gotten myself into. Again," I said, pondering my life, trying to read, and write notes. I was glad to have him to give me comfort and courage to press forward, regardless of my fears.

Gold phoned again, demanding that I drop everything and drive in solely for supervision.

"I'm not coming in today," I repeated. "I didn't schedule. I'm getting supervision from Brenda, as I said. I refuse to pay for something I didn't ask for." I wondered if I could make it stick. I knew it was easier to give in, because Gold would try every angle until he got me to give him money. He wouldn't hesitate to confront me in front of my clients. He'd done that before and embarrassed me into paying. He'd open the door to my office during a session and say, "Tommy, I know you're having financial problems, but be sure to leave me your check today." Or "Tommy, don't forget you owe me for your last supervision." He knew I wouldn't want to argue in front of my clients, who would draw back at least internally. To get him out of my office, I'd write him a check and hand it over.

I hung up the phone and went back to my paperwork and reading.

Half an hour later, Gold called again, his voice full of humility. "Tommy, I'm afraid I must have mixed you up with another Tom who's a client of mine. I'd like to take you out to lunch to make things up to you."

I listened. I had never heard of a Tom who was a client. Despite rules of confidentiality, Gold wasn't one to keep silent about his clients' names or their troubles, especially if they reeked with drama. When confronted about it, he'd say, "Such rules don't apply to those who are members of a psychotherapy practice. I specialize in ethics. I know."

"You name the day, Tommy," he said, his voice on the other end of the line sounding repentant. "I won't push so hard. I know you're under stress with publication deadlines. Being a therapist isn't your first priority."

When I met Gold for lunch the following week—on his suggestion—he took me to a new restaurant in the new white Audi Cabriolet convertible he'd just leased. He was Proud of the car, joking that his wife and friends said he was going through a midlife crisis.

"You probably are," I said. "But as my mom said of my dad, you've been going through midlife crises all your life."

"Did you have to say something so hurtful?" Gold asked. "It's a happy day. Birds are singing—tulips blooming. Spring is in the air. Nature rejoices."

"Knock it off, Gold. You can't say you don't ask for such remarks," I replied.

"You act like some of my nieces and nephews. When they come to our house to visit, as they just did, they tell me I need to go on a diet because I'm fat. They run behind me to see if they can get a look at my crack. They make jokes about my *Grand Canyon*."

I laughed. "Out of the mouths of babes."

Gold was in such a good mood that he didn't respond negatively.

As we approached the restaurant window, Gold spotted the head of the consulting business next door. She was sitting at a table eating lunch. "Look who's here," he whispered to me, holding the door open so I could enter first. "I heard she was going to be here. She's interested in me." He glowed. He strode toward her table to say hello. She was with a smartly dressed, coifed, and handsome man in a navy-blue, pinstripe suit. He looked in his early forties, in peak health, with little body fat, and a great tan. By comparison, Gold and I looked like we'd been sitting too long in the public library.

Gold whispered to me, "I'm glad you're along. I won't seem like a wolf on the hunt."

I merely raised my eyebrow. "The truth comes out," I said. I swore he was drooling.

With his usual brassy warmth, Gold said, "Hello Katherine, it is *so* good to run into you."

Perfunctorily, she said, "Hello," then returned to her conversation with her lunch partner.

"You remember my colleague, Dr. Watson, don't you," Gold asked, refusing to take the hint.

"Yes, hello," Katherine said, glancing at me, then back at her partner. Clearly she wanted the man with her to know that he was her center of attention. She looked entranced.

"That bitch! She's led me along for months," Gold fumed, storming away from Katherine's table. "I've lost my appetite. Let's get out of here."

"But I'm hungry. I didn't eat breakfast so I could splurge at lunch."

"I can't eat. The bitch has given me a gut ache," Gold said, stomping to the door.

As we walked to the Audi, Gold remained unusually quiet.

"Are you sure she led you along?" I asked. "I've never seen any evidence of it."

"What would you know? You aren't sexual."

"I have eyes. I've never seen her display any serious interest in you. She's been friendly but never excessively so."

The anger was visible in Gold's set jaw and down-turned brows. His jowls vibrated with rage.

"You deceive yourself, Gold," I said. "I've seen it many times in the ambitious. You think you can bag anyone who takes your fancy. When people don't fall into your clutches, it's their fault. They're cold. They're distant, heavily defended. They aren't sexual. They're gay. They're lesbian." I paused. "The truth is—people just aren't interested."

"Your friend Helen," he fumed, changing the subject. "I'm planning to make her resign. No one likes her. She's getting bitchier all the time. She doesn't hesitate to talk back in front of clients and other therapists. She refuses to do the assignments I give her." Suddenly Gold decided to stop at the Tattered Cover Bookstore before returning to the office. Taking a sharp right into the parking building next to the store, he screeched through the alleys and up the ramps to successive floors, searching for a parking spot. "I've found we can hire a nubile high school junior under the school's work-study program. She's cute, very bright, and responsive, with perky little breasts and manner. She's Rubinesque. I could reach out and pinch those cheeks every time I see her," he added, his mood warming, as his hands pinched the air before him. "What more could we ask? We'll save a lot of money."

"Not that we pay Helen a fortune," I said. Gold didn't even pay her health insurance. She got a couple of dollars over minimum wage. I opposed him on all those points, but it made no difference. Gold got what he wanted.

Despite his search, Gold found no parking spot. He drove down again to the lower level and then back up to the top, still looking. There on the upper level, he spotted a very narrow space next to the railing that protected the windows of the Tattered Cover Bookstore from errant cars.

"That isn't a parking spot," I said. "There are no lines."

"I can get in it," Gold said. He slowed down to maneuver. He couldn't make it without scratching the car. He backed up and began all over, creeping forward.

"If you do get the car in, we won't be able to get out," I warned.

"We'll see about that. I know how to work my way into tight spots. That's the way I like them, tight and virginal. I'll have that bitch next door before I'm finished. You watch."

"Oh, so this is some Freudian display of masculine outrage over rejection?" I asked. It was Gold who had alerted me to the truth that so many of the ambitious who rise to the top of their fields are "seed droppers," as he called them. He meant that they liked to screw everyone whom they could get their hands on. I'd never put such facts together before.

With a long grunt, Gold pushed his way into the tight spot. I couldn't open my door. He couldn't open his.

"Climb out the back," Gold ordered, managing to lift himself out of the seat. He lumbered back and over the trunk. Once standing on the cement, he pulled up his pants, which had fallen below his buttocks and were on the way down.

"You didn't ask how my keynote address to the State Association of Social Workers went last week," he said, breathing hard but brightening.

Managing to get my foot freed from the seat, I then made it over the trunk and jumped down. "Maybe I didn't care," I said, following as he ambled over to the fourth-floor door of the Tattered Cover. "You, Mister," I called to Gold, "need to get some serious therapy. Do not hesitate a moment longer."

"I was the star of the convention," Gold said, letting the door slam in my face.

He was active in many local organizations. He wrote good articles and was an engaging speaker—when he spent adequate time preparing and focusing on the task.

Inside the store, he picked up a marked-down book and leafed through the pages." I thought you'd like to know I'm becoming an Anglican," Gold announced. "I'd hoped to be accepted into full communion on Pentecost, but I have to go through catechumen classes before they'll baptize me." He paused. "My Jewish friends think I've had a psychotic break," he added. With a laugh, he tossed both the notion and the book down.

"Nothing would surprise me," I said, noticing how shaky I was starting to feel from not eating all day.

"You're so vicious these anymore," Gold lamented, sounding hurt and about to cry. "I've always wanted to be baptized and join the church for Emma's sake."

"But she isn't an Anglican."

"No, Emma's a Catholic," Gold said. "Becoming an Anglican will make her happy. It's close." He paused, trying to sound extra sincere and warm. "I'm getting more interested in spirituality, especially with people like you around."

My experiences with Gold were becoming more and more surreal. I could have laughed—if only I'd been watching him on a movie screen instead of experiencing him in real life.

I Saw Eternity

The president of our Homeowners' Association resigned. Three years before, he'd moved to Greeley but still kept his office and managed the townhomes from there. In February he'd sold his unit to the woman who had been renting it from him.

An HOA, Homeowners' Association, meeting was called. Officers were elected. Ron Riva, active in the local business community, was elected our president. As things traditionally stood, this meant he would also manage the HOA.

After the election, Rita, Ron's wife, started sending out memos and acting on her husband's behalf.

Another HOA meeting was called in the common area behind our units. Rita opened. "I called this meeting to discuss the dog policies and the yard." Her husband couldn't make the meeting. She was acting in his stead.

Before anyone else spoke, our new neighbor, Jessie, said, "I believe we all should thank Tom for giving us such beautiful gardens." She set a couple of bottles of wine and some glasses out on the picnic table where homeowners were gathered. She'd recently bought the unit next door to me and moved her two kids, cat, dog, and new husband in with her. "Everyone, please help yourself to a glass," Jessie said. "I see Tom out working in the gardens every day. His dog helps him."

I felt a chill in the air. It emanated from Rita. She intended to share the spotlight with no one.

Everyone poured a glass—everyone except Rita. "Aren't you joining us?" Jessie asked, pouring a glass of wine for Rita. She tried to hand it to her.

Rita pushed it away. "I don't drink."

"How long have you been sober?" Jessie asked.

Breaking a deadly silence, Twila, one of our original townhome owners, remarked, "The gardens have never looked this good." She now lived off-site with her husband and new baby. When I'd first bought my townhome, people who lived there got together regularly for spontaneous potlucks in the common area. Someone would bring a bottle of wine, another, a salad or pasta, and someone else a dessert or whatever, and invite others to join in. Since Denver's weather was usually mild, we had outside potlucks most of the year, especially in summer. Twila added, "Bob (the former president of the HOA) walked the grounds every day."

"Why would he do that?" Rita asked.

"Because he really cared about the place," Twila responded in her friendly way. "He was pro-active."

"He loved the task," I said. "When I moved back into my place, he said he'd see I got paid for my gardening. He was still managing from Greeley. He appreciated my dedication and expertise. I told him I wasn't really concerned about getting paid, since I wanted the gardens to look good."

Rita said, "We don't have all day. We need to move on."

"We need more wood chips on the gardens," I said, sitting on the picnic table bench, while Baltho sat on the cobbled walk beside me. "Having to hand water most of the gardens is a chore. I suggest we install a drip system. I'd be glad to do it. I've looked around at the materials. It looks pretty easy. You use push-on connections and porous hoses attached to timers on the two spigots in back. We'll save a lot of money on water because we won't have any evaporation. No water is wasted on the cobbled walks or the building."

"I don't think we need to spend the money," Rita said. "We should to put this project on hold."

"We'll spend some money, maybe a few hundred dollars in supplies, but we'll save more on water, even the first year," I said. "I'll do the work for free." Most of the water came from my unit, with some coming from the unit on the alley, which had belonged to our former HOA president. We two homeowners had to submit our water bills and then get reimbursed for water usage above what we used in the winter. That was considered our base rate. So I knew how much summer water was costing us.

"I think we should wait," Rita repeated, moving the meeting along to the next item on the agenda. "Tom has requested a three-hundred dollar a year allowance for plants, fertilizer, and garden materials."

Baltho decided to get up and check out the eight-foot high privacy fence that ran along the alley. Squirrels often scampered along the top of it, carrying food they'd scrounged from the dumpster. Sometimes they'd drop something that a dog could snap up. Often the squirrels would stop and look down at the animal below, tempting it to fly up and grab them. I could imagine Baltho's hope that a squirrel would someday misstep and land at his feet. "See what I've bagged for you!" he'd telegraph, holding it beneath his paws as he did on the first day we were together.

After some discussion, I was granted my three-hundred dollar a year gardening allowance. Not much, but I could stay within budget, especially when I also bought bulbs and plants myself.

"I still don't think the three hundred dollar gardening allowance is necessary," Rita said, although the motion had cleared. She'd been the only one to object. "By the way, anyone who wants to buy things and turn in the receipts is welcome to do so. This isn't Tom's domain alone."

After a little more chitchat, Rita said that she and Ron wanted "to raise the pay we get each month for management from seventy-five to a hundred dollars. It's a lot of work."

Her request was granted.

"You can get plants cheaper at K Mart than shopping at the local greenhouses and Costco," Rita said to me. She refused to let the subject of my allowance go.

"I've tried K Mart plants," I said. "Costco can't be beat. Nor can Eliot's Gardens, or Dardano's. I drive all around town looking for the best deals. Besides, if you're going to pay someone to come in and mow each week, you ought to pay me, since I work in the yard every day, even in the winter."

"You don't do any more than a couple of other owners," Rita said. "Besides, you love gardening. It's your hobby."

I saw Twila and Jessie raise their eyebrows. "He's often out working at dawn," Jessie said. Her manner was breezy. "But you have to get up early to see him."

Baltho left the fence at the back and walked up to Rita. He sat down quietly beside her and stared at up her. She looked down. He continued to stare. She reached down and pushed him away. "Tom, put your dog in the house," she said. "With you, your dog, and Jessie's menagerie, I feel like we've been invaded."

"I'll go get Sproing," Jessie said, referring to her often wild hunting dog. "If you want to know what it's like to feel invaded, he'll show you."

I got up and took Baltho inside. I remained indoors. Dealing with controlling and illogical people was taking a toll. This meeting was about to finish anyway, and I doubted that much would get done after I left. They'd talk about dogs running around unattended and decide once again to issue an order that they had to be accompanied by their owner. "Violators will be fined," they'd say, although it wouldn't happen.

I had no problem with that. Despite such rules, some people dumped their dogs outside. Some of the dogs were well-behaved. Some liked to dig holes in the gardens and lie in them. If I didn't fill them in, and try to replant the vegetation that had been dug out, the holes would soon grow bigger and engulf everything.

I decided to lie down on my bed for a nap. The bedroom was comfortable. I felt Baltho jump up beside me. I hugged him like a giant hairy rag doll. Before long, Figgy was lying on the other side of me. I felt and heard him purring loudly against the small of my back.

In a little while, I woke with a start. Sweating profusely, I was overcome with grief. It came through again. Almost always now I remembered to avoid wrestling with Baltho because I couldn't stand the anguish it brought.

I jumped off the bed, with Baltho and Figgy following. It was late in the afternoon. I told Baltho and Figgy, "We need to make dinner. There's a nice chicken thawed in the refrigerator. We'll bake it and have a bite to eat. Then Baltho and I will go out for a long walk, while Figgy takes a good nap."

When Baltho and I walked later, I told him not to worry. "I know for good reason you aren't fond of Rita. By her logic, people shouldn't be compensated for the things they love, not even for the expense of running around town for plants and materials. If you dislike your duties, then you must be paid." Baltho stopped, looked up at me, and let out a big sigh. "But, we have to try to live with one another."

When Baltho got up and began walking again, I noticed he wasn't galloping or racing ahead of me as he used to. Although I'd tried not to pay attention to this new custom, I now couldn't help it. He'd been with me for nearly a year. Nor was he cantering like a horse. That night he seemed to lumber. He lagged behind, like an aging dog. Surely, he was no more than seven or eight years old.

Even with regular walks, Baltho had managed to put on weight, slowly, steadily. I fed him good food, low fat, with no junk snacks. I was careful not to give him huge chews that could expand in his stomach and kill him. He could have as many raw carrots as he wanted. They were good for his teeth and gums, and made him feel full.

Perhaps, I reasoned, Baltho plodded along because it was getting warmer, and he was several pounds overweight.

Maybe he'd had enough racing along and wanted to smell the roses, or something like that. He didn't seem to be falling ill. Whenever he got the chance, he was eager to go for rides in the car. He never turned down the opportunity for a walk. He still woke early and insisted that I take him outside so he could look around and I could garden.

But I worried about getting in at least thirty minutes of power-walking or more each day for the sake of our health and hearts. More and more on the long walks, I had to remind him that we needed to keep our pace up for awhile. Then we could slow down.

This dog and I were bonded, connected as strongly as any human and dog could be. I often wondered if the reason was that we'd been together in some other life. I wasn't certain I believed in reincarnation, but I couldn't disbelieve it either. Perhaps our spirits had linked up in another dimension, one that most people don't perceive.

On occasion, I had vowed that I would give my life in exchange for a human friend, if it were possible. I'd read of such exchanges and believed them feasible. God had never chosen to take me up on that offer. For Baltho, I would do the same. Life for life. He would have done that for me. I knew it because he was always ready to defend us from attack. One of my sisters would care for him if the divine plan called for my life in exchange for his.

I was scared that I was going to lose this dog, my own Mr. Dog, my Baltho.

I looked up. Despite the glare of city lights, the sky was ablaze with stars. I thought of the 17th century English poet, Henry Vaughan, and his poem, "The World."

> I saw eternity the other night
> Like a great ring of pure and endless light,

"Come, Mr. Dog. It's time to go home," I said. He turned, and, at a steady but moderate pace, we headed back.

The Power

Baltho, Figgy, and I greeted my mom, my youngest sister Vickie, her husband, Tim, and their two children, eight-year-old Kelsie and five-year-old Kyle, at the front door. Suitcases in hand, they were going to spend the weekend.

I told my mom we'd put her upstairs in my room, "unless you want to sleep on the living room floor with the rest of us."

"I could do without it," Mother said, to Kelsie and Kyle's cry of "Oh Grandma, you're such a party pooper!" She knew we were giving her a hard time. Her bad back wouldn't permit sleeping on the floor. "Baltho, mind your manners!" she said, pushing his nose away.

"You know he's just trying to wake you up," I said, laughing.

"Go wake Tom up," she ordered, pushing Baltho toward me. "He owns his sexuality," she added.

"He wakes me up all the time, usually just before dawn, especially in the summer," I joked. I turned serious, "Truth is, Baltho knows that I want to be awake. You don't, except physically."

My sister changed the subject by bringing up our plans for that night.

"Gold is having one of his famous 'soirees,' as he calls them," I said. "As summer approaches, he gets especially revved up. The food and wine will be good, with lots of intelligent and interesting people. Never mind that a dozen will be counselees," I said, half-joking.

"Isn't that against the law?" Tim asked.

"He's an ethics specialist. He's a law unto himself."

We decided to go out for dinner and then return for our sleep-out. It was too early to leave for the restaurant, so we continued chitchatting.

"Grandma gets the dog," Kyle said. "I get the cat."

"I want Baltho," Kelsie cried. "Please, Grandma! Have a heart," Kelsie pleaded.

"Don't worry," Vickie said. "You can cuddle with Baltho all night long. Grandma doesn't mind."

Kyle and Kelsie started spreading their sleeping bags out on the carpet.

"You know what will happen if you do that, don't you?" I asked. "Baltho and Figgy will claim them as their own while we're gone."

They glanced at each other and continued. They went on to spread out their mother's and dad's sleeping bags.

"This way Baltho and Figgy can have their choice," Kelsie said, smiling. "Uncle Tom, where's your sleeping bag?"

"I'll have to use blankets. I don't have a sleeping bag."

"Mom, why didn't we bring another bag for Tom?"

"We couldn't find one of his exes," Tim said. He usually was reserved, except for the occasional wry comment.

"Tom has exes?" Kelsie asked. I pictured her imagining letters from the alphabet.

"Your dad means ex-wives," Vickie explained.

"Uncle Tom was married?" Kelsie asked.

"That was before either you or your brother was born."

"That's good," Kelsie said, happily content with the answer.

"Why's it good?" I asked.

"That way we don't have to worry about forgetting them," Kelsie said. "They're gone."

"Your uncle Tom wishes it was so easy, don't you, Uncle Tom?" Vickie asked.

"Boy, do I," I said.

"Let's change the subject," Mother said. She'd thought the first ex was fine until a week before our wedding, when she phoned to urge me to cancel the ceremony.

"It's kinda late now," I'd said. "All the plans have been made, the caterer and photographer hired, the church reserved, and the invitations sent out."

"I have a terrible feeling about it," Mother said. "It's hit me like a ton of bricks."

"Too bad you didn't have this feeling when you were so encouraging of our dating," I said.

"We've learned some things about her character. We have reason to think she used your sister Diane to get to you. She's saying terrible things about Diane to her voice teacher and mutual friends."

I hadn't known who to trust. The ex did have a habit of saying vicious things about my sister Diane, who was far from ambitious and successful. I wasn't too pleased with her myself.

But that was more than ten years ago.

"Well, I think I want to go to Gold's party," Mother said, sitting on the couch. "I need to witness more sideshows." Baltho immediately jumped up on her lap. He put his face right up into hers. She sputtered, as she'd gotten a mouth full of his hair. She tried to push him off.

Kelsie and Kyle plopped themselves down beside Mother, and called Baltho to them. He moved over to position himself across their laps. Figgy then jumped up on my mom's lap and lay down.

"Animals at home—what a portrait," my mom muttered, petting Figgy.

"We'll take a picture and have it blown up and captioned, *Animals at Home*," I said. "We can all have framed copies to hang over our couches."

"Your animals are quieter than Diane's and Grandma's," Kyle said.

"That's for sure," Kelsie added. "Later, Grandma is going to put on her dress so Baltho and she can play elevator nose. Then we can all watch."

I laughed.

Mother groaned.

"Baltho is a therapy dog," I said. "He is helping Grandma straighten out her mind and discover her true self." I tried hard to keep a straight face.

"I sure as heck don't need Baltho to help me discover anything," Mother grumbled.

The phone rang. I answered. Gold was on the other end. "I want to make sure you're coming tonight. I know your family members are in town. Bring them. Just bring some extra bottles of wine and don't forget that big salad."

"I don't think we'll make it, as I already told you." I hung up the phone.

The phone rang again. My family urged me not to answer. "We know who it is," Kelsie shouted.

"It's the monster that ate the world!" Kyle said, running to the kitchen to turn off the answering machine.

The phone rang and rang and rang. We counted sixteen rings.

"What if it's an emergency?" I asked. "Sometimes that happens. I don't think it's good not to be able to screen calls," I said, walking to the kitchen to turn on the machine again. The phone stopped ringing.

Then the phone started in again. This time we let the machine pick it up.

"I forgot to tell you—Betty's quit our group," Gold said. "She won't be doing any medical supervision or advising, starting the first of the month."

I was tempted to call back and ask for more information, but my family talked me into letting it wait. "He's probably trying to find another way to get you to come in and pay him," my mom suggested. By then, Baltho had turned around and had his head back resting on her lap alongside Figgy, who was still there. Kelsie and Kyle had the rest of Baltho's body on theirs. They were performing like good little children, petting away.

"Yep, animals at home," I said, laughing.

"Just what we need," Mother said.

I looked at her and smiled. "Speaking of aberrations," I began, "what's the latest with your pastor?"

"Did I tell you that he visited the school where I teach and saw a prayer to the Great Spirit on the door of my colleague Sharon?" Vickie asked.

I shook my head. "No," I said.

"He ripped it down and marched it to the principal, demanding an apology and the promise that prayers that weren't Christian wouldn't be allowed in school," Vickie said.

"He fails to recognize anything but his own narrow brand of Christianity as valid," I said.

"He's immature," Mother said.

"I don't know why you always want to minimize his aberrations," I said. "He's worse than immature."

"Do you know he wasn't willing to let it go?" Vickie asked. "Our principal told him that we enjoy freedom to teach about different cultures in America. The Great Spirit was the Indians' name for God, the same God that all of us worship," Vickie related. "Well, he went to the school board and demanded that they fire both Sharon and the principal."

"Let the burnings begin," I muttered. "You really think he's merely immature?" I asked, turning directly to my mom.

She avoided answering.

"He wants Grandma to kick you out of the family," Kelsie said, her manner matter-of-fact.

"You need to find a new church," I said.

"Do you want me to gather some women together who will make placards and stand outside the church in protest?" Mother asked.

"Great idea, Mother! I might be able to return home in that case. After all these years, I would be so proud of you," I exclaimed, beaming. "My Mother is finally standing up for truth and justice. Then you can work on getting unyoked from Diane."

Tellingly, Baltho lifted his head, let out a long sigh of exclamation, and placed his nose on Mother's bosom. Pressing in, he looked adoringly up at her.

She winced but stroked his head like a good mother.

I laughed. So did the rest of the family.

When we got back from dinner at The New Saigon Restaurant, I found a little present on my doorstep. It was a package of mixed flavor dog treats, all heart-shaped. The gift card was signed, "Love, Susanna."

"Oh wonderful," I said, "she just can't leave things alone." Several months before, I'd agreed to meet briefly with Susanna, who was looking for a therapist. She'd never been married and desired help finding a mate. During the introductory session, it became apparent that she'd be difficult—far beyond my skills.

She'd wanted to meet with me at my home, but, even from our phone conversation, I knew better.

"All the potential mates I meet are gay," Susanna complained, plunking herself down on the couch directly in front of my chair. She worked as a singing waitress in an uptown restaurant, where the wait staff sang arias. She began singing *Un Bel Di* in a small, ethereal voice.

"Why do you suppose that's the case?" I asked.

"They're all actors, for God's sake. Men are actors in general, but these are *gay* actors." She crossed her legs at the ankle and gave me a tight smile. "Now, you're a man I can admire—highly intelligent, verbal, talented—a real Christian," Susanna said, leaning forward.

I wondered how she'd come up with that assessment of me.

"Blushing is so becoming on that pink dimpled cheek of yours," she said, raising herself so she could reach to pinch my cheek.

I drew back. She was about to cross the line, so I asked about her childhood.

"I've been in therapy for years. I was sexually abused by a Satanic cult, beginning when I was two or three years old," she said. Her tone and manner remained matter of fact.

Everyone had been reading about ritual abuse, though many questioned the notion that it was so widespread as some asserted. The growing rage for ritual abuse treatment seemed too trendy for my tastes. Because many lives could be wrecked by unfounded allegations, I saw yellow caution lights everywhere.

"I had a great therapist in Seattle. That gal is excellent," Susanna gushed. "She has a huge clientele with a waiting list over a year long. She uses hypnosis to reach the memories we've repressed and heal the trauma associated with them."

I'd been interested in hypnosis for decades, so I wondered how careful her therapist was to avoid leading her clients. Implanting memories is all too easy. So is leading one's clients.

"She puts us under hypnosis, and we remember everything—the black candles, the robes, the incense and altars—the chants, the abuse. We relive it to heal it."

I had the distinct impression that Susanna's love of drama was coming through.

"The cult abused many, many in the entire state of Washington and beyond. We're working on a class action lawsuit against them now. They put curses on us."

I glanced over at the clock on my desk. We'd been talking for half an hour. This was an initial consultation. "Susanna, I'm not the right therapist for you. I want you to find a good therapist in Denver who specializes in ritual abuse. I'd suggest a female, given your issues."

"I want you to be my therapist," she said. "I saw the one in Seattle three or four times a week. I'm sure I need that. I'll pay you."

"How many years did she see you?" I asked, thinking of the expenses that she'd incurred. Every authority I'd read says therapists should refer difficult cases to someone else, rather than treating them for years.

"Oh ten, maybe eleven years," Susanna answered.

I'm sure I looked shocked because Susanna assured me that she knew herself "much, much better as a result. I'm oodles more stable than I used to be. The shackles are coming off."

I shifted in my chair but tried to show little reaction. "I just don't have the training for your case."

When she finally left my office, Susanna waved goodbye with her usual dramatic flair. "Think about it. I'm sure you'll do just fine."

"Oh, no I won't," I whispered, once behind my closed office door. After she left, I did some research and wrote a letter to her, recommending three local female therapists who specialized in sex abuse issues, including ritual abuse. They were said to be solid, although I knew none of them personally.

Susanna then started driving by my house, dropping off little presents—a small houseplant, some dog treats, a couple of dog toys. I did exactly as Gold advised and ignored her. I refused to open the door. I didn't take her calls. If I mistakenly answered the phone, I told her, "I cannot talk with you. You do not respect my boundaries. You are not my client. I lack the training to see you. You must find another therapist trained in ritual abuse."

On the answering machine, Susanna had left a message while my family and I were gone. "I'm so sorry I missed you. You must be out having a good time with someone. I peeked in your window and saw your precious dog. He was sleeping with a cat. How adorable. I love sleeping with big hairy animals myself."

"Who in the heck is that?" Vickie asked.

"She sounds like Diane," Tim said.

"She sounds like we should change the subject," I concluded.

Get Outta Here

Marty called me into the work room. We were alone. He closed the door and spoke softly. It was the end of July. The temperature of the room rose quickly. "According to Gold, Betty quit us because of you. She says you're green and unethical."

My jaw dropped. Gold had never said a word to me about this. I was pretty certain it wasn't true. "No wonder everyone's been cutting me a wide berth," I said. "I thought my deodorant wasn't working."

Marty laughed. "You know you can't believe more than twenty percent of what Gold says."

"If that."

Marty shrugged. "I thought I'd better tell you, since he's spreading it all around as fact."

"She told me she'd continue to give me medical supervision as needed, so I doubt that she wants to distance herself from me."

Marty laughed, as if letting me in on a secret. "She's told me she'll continue to supervise me too."

"Seems pretty clear that it's Gold she's had enough of."

Marty nodded. "She's been indicating that for years. At some point, people finally get fed up."

I marched back to Gold's office. He was sitting at his desk, skimming Bly's *Iron John*. Once he'd picked up a few key concepts, he'd claim to have read it. "I hear you're saying that Betty quit because of me. I don't like being blamed for something that isn't true. Evidently, you don't think your bullshit will ever catch up with you."

"I don't lie." Gold took off his readers and stood. Pulling his shoulders back he turned to stare me down. "Bullshit is lying."

"You're full of it—bullshit, lies, manure, and everything like it," I said, storming out of his office to the waiting area.

"What an ass," I said to Helen, who nodded.

She called me over to tell me that Marty had been turned down for life insurance. A few months before, she and I had both noticed a strange patch of hair about the size of a nickel at the back of his head. It had turned white and seemed to get larger. "He's been complaining of fatigue for months," she said. "But he's never said anything else about his health."

I shrugged. "He's never said anything to me."

Helen pushed a returned letter on her desk toward me. It had been incorrectly addressed. "You might want to see this," she said. Inside, was brochure for the men's film group that Gold and I had not long before planned to facilitate together. Over twelve weeks, we were going to view and discuss a classic film, centering on men's issues. The film would serve as a spring-board for group therapy. The idea had been mine.

"I'll be a co-facilitator," Gold had said, jumping on the notion. I did the planning, chose the films, and wrote up the brochures, which I had printed.

Inside, was a note from Gold to the head of the counseling program at one of our local seminaries. "You might be interested in this innovative therapy group centering on men's issues, which I have designed. Spirituality will be thoroughly explored."

"How'd this note get in there?" I asked.

"Gold wanted it tucked in all mailings to various program directors in the area," Helen said.

I handed the materials back to her. "I guess it's a good thing we cancelled." Only twelve men had signed up.

"Gold didn't see any money in it, after all," Helen remarked. She tossed the materials into the trash can.

The next time I talked with Marty, I asked how he was. I mentioned the white patch of hair. "I wonder if it isn't on some meridian that signals a problem you need to attend to," I said.

"Oh it's just some freak of nature," Marty joked, "like me."

I urged him to ask his acupuncturist. "If I remember, I'll ask mine."

He walked back to his office.

Helen voiced her opinion. "To die is the only way he'll break free of Gold's control," she whispered. "Mark my words."

The thought upset me.

"For some reason, Gold has him under his thumb." She shifted directions. "I know Gold wants me to resign, but I won't do it until I'm good and ready. I know the game," she said. "I've worked for lawyers."

As I left the offices, I tried not to worry about Marty—or about Helen. I looked forward to spending time with my dog. Even if he couldn't walk a long way now, he wanted to be near. He loved me, no matter what.

Yet, the notion that Marty's health was in danger haunted me. Marty had been with the Golds for years.

More than once, Gold had bragged how he'd helped Marty shake his drinking and come to grips with his homosexuality. Typically he added, "Marty's loyal. He'll be with us for years."

I thought about Marty's being turned down for life insurance. Something serious was wrong.

I started the car. Dionne Warwick's rendition of Bacharach and David's "A House Is Not a Home" was playing on the radio. When Warwick got to the lines about opening the door and seeing the face of her beloved, I thought of Mr. Dog. He would be there waiting for me. He turned my house into a home, gave me a reason to live, to press forward, no matter what.

My eyes teared up so badly that I couldn't pull out into traffic. To feel like that over a dog seemed kind of crazy. Yet I knew it was true.

And the Glory

It was September twelfth. Some friends of the Episcopal parish that I had belonged to for years before moving the base of my campus ministry to the Cathedral had invited me to an end-of-summer cookout in the mountains. I asked if I could take Baltho. He had been part of my family for a year and two months.

"Of course—Magi Balthazar is always welcome," the host said. "So are you."

Even though lots had happened since I'd last seen most of the people from my old parish, I looked forward to seeing them again.

The host, Brian, and his wife Laura's new home was situated up above Nederland in stream-watered meadows surrounded by mountains. No other homes stood near theirs.

As I drove into the gravel drive, I noticed a number of friends from my former parish standing about. When Baltho jumped down from the car, he transformed. He became like the dog I'd known the year before—more agile and energetic than the dog who accompanied me now. At first, he trotted around near me, greeting people. Soon, he decided to prance further, seeking attention on his own.

I was glad to see him acting so much better. Perhaps the summer heat and air pollution got him down, just as they did me. The weather in the mountains was clear, cool, and crisp. I surveyed the landscape. The hills were awash with fall asters, pink, white, and lavender. A killing frost would come at any time.

I noticed a number of people out on the patio chuckling and laughing about "the wise guy." I walked out into the sun. I had to shade my eyes to see what was going on. Baltho had helped himself not just to one bratwurst on the grill, but he'd just gone back for another. He was unafraid of the often-flaming embers, sure of his ability to snatch a brat without getting burned or lighting his massive beard on fire.

Just as I apologized, one of the men tossed Baltho another bratwurst.

"Please don't feed him any more of those," I said. "Anybody got a birthday cake?" asked one of my friends who knew the story of the Afghans and the birthday cake "Put it on top of the refrigerator. We'll know that he's really doing well if we catch him up there slurping it down."

"Oh that's what happened to Julie, wasn't it?" Laura remarked. "It was such a funny story. She caught her two Afghans up on top of the refrigerator on tiptoe, slurping down the cake she'd made for her husband's birthday."

I remembered Julie. She had also been a member of the parish until she and her husband moved to Seattle.

"Don't give him more!" I yelled, just as someone began to feed him another bratwurst. "I'm afraid they'll make him sick. He's not used to all that fat."

"Have you heard that I resigned as the Christian Ed Director?" Brian asked.

"No, I hadn't heard. Why?" I asked.

He drew me aside. "I was always afraid someone would accuse me of molesting one of the kids."

"Well, when you teach your little daughter anatomically correct terms—and she names her anatomically correct girl doll Drina, because she thinks that's what girls have, so it also becomes the name of her new doll—I can imagine what ideas you might stir up," I said, desperately needing to draw a big breath. "That sentence was so long I need oxygen." I coughed, then laughed.

Laura had slipped over to stand at Brian's side. I hadn't seen either of them for months. I took Baltho over to their home down in Denver soon after I found him, but our lives moved more and more in different directions. Laura reminded me, "You wanted to get Lili an anatomically correct boy doll so she could call him Enis."

"I remember." I smiled. "She thought I was her monkey-bar set, climbing all over me."

"She took a real liking to you," Laura said.

I was reminded how their son had decided to climb under my legs and hold on, as if attached, when I was trying to kneel on the bed to help her hang a picture on the wall behind it.

"Our kids both really liked you," Laura said. "It's so hard to think that Clive has already graduated from college and Lili will soon graduate from high school."

"I'll have to find Lili an Enis for graduation," I said. "I'll search eBay."

"Please don't," Laura said. "She'd be embarrassed."

"No, her friends would think it was hilarious," Brian said.

"So, why did you really quit your position?" I asked.

"The politics of Christianity are overwhelming. It's all us versus them nowadays. The churches have gone from being apolitical to being overly political."

"We've left the church," Laura added.

I stood back, a little surprised. Baltho stopped his meandering out in the wildflowers and came to stand beside me. I reached down to pat his head.

"After discovering the philandering of so many ministers, mostly married—with men and with women—we decided we'd had it," Laura said.

"You too," I commented. "I just don't expect pastors to screw the sheep, both literally and metaphorically," I said. I paused, and then continued. "I don't have any friends now who are involved in any church, no matter what branch of Christianity. We haven't necessarily given up our faith."

"I've always had a hard time believing in anything beyond the here and now," Brian reminded me. I'd known him since undergraduate days. Laura was a few years younger than both of us.

"How come you believe, Tom?" Laura asked.

"I think it's because I'm a mystic. My experiences make the divine real, but not narrowly defined or dogmatic."

"I don't know why we didn't believe you when you told us about the Dean of the Cathedral," Brian said. "We thought you were making things up because you were mad at him."

I then remembered why things between us had changed. I expected more from my friends, especially ones who had known me for half our lives. "I was mad at the Dean because he showed himself to be opposite of what a man of God should be," I said. "He cut me off when I urged him to seek therapy. When I tried to talk with others around him, they acted as if they had no idea what I was talking about. They made me feel guilty for daring to besmirch someone in his position. Yet, the evidence was everywhere."

"People never seem to learn," Laura said.

"I'll bet you miss university life in general," Brian said.

"Yes," I said. "I liked being a campus chaplain. It suited me because college chaplaincies encourage exploration. So should the church."

"It's just too bad the church could never come up with a salary," Laura lamented.

"The Dean of the Cathedral promised he would," I reminded them. "That's why I moved my ministry base there." I felt the weight of the past more clearly. "I loved being a professor even more."

"Lots of people knew about your Chair. He also wrecked lots of lives. Why didn't the university stop him?" Laura asked.

I felt Baltho press his head up against my hand. "The Ombudsperson said little could be done because he was one of the most powerful people on campus. She promised to speak on my behalf, and call it a personality conflict, but we never got that far. People trust the one in authority. He says it—they believe him—and that's that. They seldom probe further."

"So you get screwed because you wouldn't be probed by your Chair or Cathedral Dean," Brian quipped.

I caught a whiff of the meats cooking on the barbeque. "The burgers and bratwursts are making me hungry." I hoped to shift our conversation to something happier.

"When I was first born again," Brian said, "everyone tried to love one another." He hugged Laura to him. "We were earnest about our call to be seekers of truth and live out justice and mercy," Brian continued. "We knew we were supposed to lead upright lives, being salt and light, not smashing and grabbing shadows of deceit."

"Oh Tom, I'm so sad!" Laura exclaimed, sounding as if she was about to cry. Her look was devastating. "Remember how hopeful we used to be, how committed to God? We really believed in the power of goodness!" she exclaimed. "What happened?"

Her reminders made me sad too. I felt the sky like a mill stone pressing down and beginning to turn. Baltho was leaning against my leg. I patted his head. "Trying to steady me, aren't you, Mr. Dog."

Indicating that we had to move away from the pain, he let out a happy bark and galloped off into the meadows to chase a white butterfly that had flown by his nose. "Mr. Dog calls," I said and took off, following some yards behind.

Laura and Brian called, "See ya," and remained where they were.

Even through high grasses, I could track Baltho by his curved tail moving along. I wasn't going to attempt to keep up with him. He seemed to have regained all the energy that I'd been afraid he'd lost.

As we passed one of the ridges, a vista of lavender-blue penstemons and lavender fall asters opened before us. They were breathtaking. In their midst, lay a beautiful large pond with cattails and grasses ringing the edges.

Baltho took one look, jumped into the water, and splashed around. He barked joyfully, reminding me of our first summer. The water looked pristine, fed by a mountain stream. No goose droppings or slime anywhere.

After a half hour, which passed quickly, Baltho emerged, shaking his hair wildly. Filthy water even hit me. Filled with joy, he barked and barked.

Now that he'd given me another shower, he seemed ready to return to the party.

People were cleaning up, but someone shouted, "We saved you a plate!"

"I'm sorry," I said, realizing how long we'd been gone. "Baltho and I were caught up in joy."

"We don't expect either you or Baltho to conform to social norms," one of the guests remarked. Others smiled benignly.

"He is my significant other," I said, knowing friends understood.

"His love is more precious to Tom than that of women," one of my old minister friends said, echoing the Bible's remarks on David's relationship with Jonathan.

Baltho sat gracefully in our midst, his eyes shining, basking in all the attention.

Brian told the story of Gold's taking Baltho into the restaurant under the pretext that he was a service dog in training.

"I forgot I told you about that," I said.

"An Afghan seeing-eye hound," Laura laughed. "I can just imagine what would happen to the poor blind person when Baltho sighted something to run after. He'd get his arm torn off."

"Heck, that can happen even when you're sighted," I said. I reached to pet Baltho's head, as he had come to stand beside me. I felt something on my thigh and looked down. Baltho had wrapped his tail, monkey-like, around it.

A woman I didn't know approached carrying a plate bristling with chips, potato salad, baked beans, and a thick hamburger on a sesame seed bun. She handed the plate to me. "I'm sure you're starving."

I realized how shaky I was feeling. I thanked her and tucked in. I felt like crying. I was reminded how much the kindness of others means.

God comes to us in many ways. Hindus say that Shiva dances, and, in dancing, Shiva destroys. But, from that destruction, creation takes place again.

Siren's Songs

I had talked briefly with a woman named Penelope at Brian and Laura's party in the mountains. I'd known her from the past, but at the party she'd made such a small impression that I'd forgotten chatting with her. Evidently, she hadn't forgotten about seeing me.

She phoned a few days later. "I'm hosting a luncheon for a small group of friends. The theme is French," she said. "I love everything about France—the food, the fashions, the sense of taste, the wine, the cheeses, the clothes." I recalled Penelope's fondness for pretension. "There'll be only a few select guests. I don't have much room, so, weather permitting, we'll sit outside on the patio. *Al fresco*, as they do in France."

I hemmed and hawed. The fall had been very warm and dry. We'd not yet had a killing frost, and it was early in November. I also remembered Penelope's voice. Shrieks lurked just below the surface. Could I endure several hours of that? I knew and liked a couple of people who'd be in attendance. I hadn't seen them for a while. I really did need to be more social. I'd hoped the counseling group would help with that, but the problems with the Golds encouraged me to withdraw into myself.

I agreed to go.

"Bring a nice bottle of red wine, French," she said. "I don't want you to bring Baltho. I don't want him disturbing my party. He's such a showoff that no one will pay attention to anything but him."

I wondered silently if Penelope's son Victor and their yellow Lab named Fifi would be there. I recalled Victor's telling me how a froufrou name had gotten tacked onto the dog he'd insisted they buy—instead of the toy poodle his mother had desired. "It was a compromise," Victor had told me. "I picked the dog. Mom picked the name. We fought a lot about it."

A few years before, Penelope had disposed of her husband. To mark the event, she had "a releasing ceremony" at the megachurch she had begun to attend. According to her, the only thing the two of them ever had in common was their son.

Brian had told me about the ceremony. "She asked me to sing. It was one of the most bizarre events I'd ever witnessed. Penelope told her husband, in so many words, eloquent as they seemed, that she was getting rid of him. He stood the whole time with a 'what in hell?' look on his face."

I'd never met her ex, but Brian said he was a genial, easygoing guy. "There was lots of singing and even a reception afterwards."

I laughed. "I'm glad I wasn't invited."

On the way over to Penelope's house, I glanced at Baltho in the rear view mirror. He was sitting in the back seat as usual, his eyes catching my gaze in the mirror. He looked happy. His face was animated. His mouth turned up a little. I knew he loved the day as much as I. I'd told him I'd slip away early and we'd go for a long walk near Penelope's. "It's November, so you won't get hot. I'll find shade, and you can stay in the car until I come back."

I began to talk with him, probably to assuage my increasing anxiety as we neared Penelope's house. "Do you think Penelope still wants to become a minister?" I asked.

"She seems to be searching for a sense of self. But I doubt that anyone would dare tell her so."

I found a nice big tree with a still-leafy canopy to park under. "I hope this event isn't going to turn into some kind of debacle." I checked my face in the mirror. Things looked ok—no spittle down the chin. "Now, I'm going to leave you in the car for maybe an hour, and then I'll be back. Be good," I said. "An hour will be quite long enough, I know."

When I arrived at Penelope's property, I walked around to the back. She had chairs arranged in a semi-circle, with several tables closing the arc. They contained plates of croissants, baguettes, pates, cheeses, and wines that looked inviting. I set my bottle of French Beaujolais on the table.

Penelope told us to help ourselves to a glass of wine. "I trust everyone has stayed with the theme and brought only French wine," she added, shooting a glance my way. "It's so much better than any other."

For a moment, I wished I'd brought a bottle of California wine. Better yet, a six-pack of Coors.

I poured a glass of Beaujolais and made small talk with a couple of guests. Penelope went to make some calls and find out where the others were.

When she returned, her face appeared pale and splotchy, in stark contrast to her jet-black hair. "I want everyone to delay eating for a little while. The other guests are probably on their way." She looked at her watch. "I told people the party was to begin at one, and it's one-thirty." She said, "People have to respect boundaries," her voice taking a turn toward a screech.

Neither of the people I'd hoped to see had arrived. Maybe they'd decided not to come.

Victor, Penelope's son, appeared. A boy of thirteen, he already stood over six-feet tall and weighed at least two-sixty. His mother fed him amply, and it showed. "Hiya,

Tom," he said, moving toward me. "Keeping busy?" he asked. Fifi, Victor's yellow Lab, walked behind him.

"Trying to," I said.

Fifi began a short run toward me. She took a leap and landed with all fours onto my chest. I caught her in my arms. "Whoa, Dog," I said. "You're lucky my reactions are quick." She licked my face profusely as I held tight to her squirming body.

In many ways, except for the licking and over-exuberance, she reminded me of Baltho. The intelligence and size were similar, although Baltho was a few inches longer and taller.

"My God, what are you doing to Fifi?" Penelope screamed. She stood a short distance away, staring with her jaw dropped. "I've never seen Fifi so out of control!"

"Fifi loves Tom," Victor said calmly, though smirking. He knew how to throw gasoline on his mother's anger. "You have Baltho in the car, don't you?" he asked, shutting out his mother's rants.

I nodded. "He's waiting patiently for me to return."

"Go get him. He should be here!"

"Your mom doesn't want him around," I said, my voice low.

"Who cares what she wants," Victor said loudly. He flipped his head back in defiance. "Go get Baltho. Fifi wants to see him. So do I."

"Tell me about your latest projects," I suggested, hoping to distract him.

Victor began telling me about his coin and rock collections—in more detail than I really cared to know. "You have to see them," he said, beckoning me into the house.

Some others, I could see, were inside. So I followed.

Victor led me to a back room where he had his collections spread out on a table. I soon realized I was standing in a bedroom, probably his. I saw bunk beds.

I glanced over his collections quickly, and then suggested we get back to the party. Knowing Penelope, I worried that she might make something of my being in her son's bedroom, even though the door was wide open. So were the curtains.

Reluctantly, Victor followed me back to the patio. He tugged at his pants because they had fallen below his belly as he walked. He straightened his shirt. I could almost hear his mother harping at him for looking disheveled and wondering why.

Most guests had now arrived. We walked to the table where cold cuts and cheeses were spread out beside a big basket of cut up baguettes. We put what we wanted on paper plates, poured wine into crystal stemware, and then sat down to eat.

"Paper plates," I thought to myself. "Penelope, Penelope, you're slipping."

I glanced at my watch. I had been there for a little over an hour. I ate some cheese and bread and drank a glass of red wine, making small talk with a few folks. Baltho was waiting patiently. I decided to make an exit.

Victor saw me get up to go. Without saying a word to me, he walked over to his mother. "I'm going to take Fifi out to see Baltho. We're going to tell him hello and goodbye."

Penelope glared at her son. She said nothing.

"I'm going to walk Baltho before driving off, Victor. I vary our routes. That way our walks don't go stale."

"I hate stale things too," Victor replied, glancing at his mother. "She's always giving me old cheese—as long as it's French. My dad calls it smegmatic."

I said nothing.

Victor insisted. "Fifi and I are going with Tom. Mom, that's all there is to it," he said. "I won't take no for an answer."

For several minutes Penelope remained splotchy-faced but silent. Finally, she gave in. It was her will or her son's. "OK, but be careful. And don't be gone long," she called, trying to control the screech that lurked behind her carefully controlled tones. Guests were present.

I assured her that we'd be back soon, "Safe, sound, and exercised. You need the workout, young man, every bit as much as Baltho and I," I said to him.

"That's what my dad says." Victor puffed his chest. "Mom just says 'eat,' so I eat. She thinks it keeps me from talking, especially mouthing off. Fat chance of that."

I laughed. Whether he realized his Freudian slips, he managed to sprinkle his remarks liberally with them. "My dad had the same idea," I said. "My sister Diane and I started our lives as children of normal weights, but soon we'd blown up like balloons. To this day, she and I are paying for it. I have to fight those fat cells every day of my life. Diane fights them, loses some weight, and then gains it—along with an additional twenty pounds—every time she diets."

Victor and Fifi followed us to the car. I carefully cracked the car door and attached the leash to Baltho's collar. I opened the door fully, and he bounded out. I was glad to see him show the enthusiasm that he used to display all the time. He went first to Victor, and then to Fifi. For a minute, they enjoyed the taste of each other's tongues and the smell of each other's behinds. "Don't tell your mom about this," I ordered. "You know she'll blame me because they act like dogs."

"Dogs in love," Victor remarked, smirking. I wasn't sure that I could trust him to keep his mouth shut.

With fast strides, we took off down the street toward Evans Avenue. "Speed up the pace, Victor." I kept an eye on Baltho, who seemed eager to go. "We want to get those heart rates up, help our hearts and circulation." As long as Baltho kept up, I intended that we do so too.

"You don't want to burn off calories?" Victor asked, with a sly smile.

"Smart ass."

"Mom doesn't like that word," Victor said.

I looked upward with a sigh. I'd supplied more infractions for him to report, if the mood took him.

Walking east, we passed a doughnut shop. "Oh good—doughnuts," Victor said, drooling. "I love doughnuts. I want one. Dad always buys me one or two. So does mom."

I resisted. "We've just had lunch. Look Victor, I know what it's like to have to fight the flab all your life. You don't want that."

"Please!" Victor begged.

"Doughnuts are one of the worst forms of junk food—grease, white flour, and fat. Not what you need."

"You're being mean," Victor screamed. "I'll tell Mom!" He refused to relent. His arms thrashed the air. He was ready to keep screaming.

Reluctantly, I left Baltho with him and Fifi, while I went to buy a jelly-filled doughnut, as he desired. If I'd let him go, I knew he'd grab more than one. He'd insisted that I buy him at least two—but I'd told him, "no way." I remembered that a Dolly Madison Ice Cream Parlor was just up the street. Ice cream was my downfall. I'd visited it sometimes when I was an undergraduate at the University of Denver. But I vowed to fight the urge. I'd just eaten.

When I returned with the doughnut, Victor grabbed it from my hand. "Thanks," he said, handing me Baltho's leash. "Too bad you didn't get me two or three." The dogs looked interested but before they could jump up, Victor had gulped it down.

We continued east toward University Boulevard. We passed the University of Denver Campus. I always liked seeing the buildings of my alma mater. When we reached the Boulevard, I said, "We'd better turn around."

Victor insisted that we go "a little further—up to Observatory Park. My dad always walks me that far."

"I'm not your dad," I said. "We ought to get back. You know your mom. I think we shouldn't delay any longer."

"She won't care," Victor insisted. "She knows you. It's broad daylight. We have our dogs. They'll protect us."

The dogs were having a good time, still pulling us along. So we walked up to Observatory Park.

"OK, this is it," I said. I began to turn around, with Baltho following my lead.

"Hey," Victor said, "I want to walk further. So does Fifi. On, Fifi!" he said, snapping the leash. She bolted. "Remember, we need to walk off those calories."

"Don't try to run everything," I yelled. I turned fully. "We're heading home."

Continuing on his own for a few yards, Victor finally gave in. He turned around, with Fifi eager to lead the way to me and Baltho. Soon, they'd caught up with us.

"You, young man, are a handful."

He laughed, but stopped acting out.

Soon, we started down the alley that led to Victor's house. We'd decided to take a short cut. We spotted Penelope standing behind her gate, waiting, as if she'd guessed where we'd be. When she saw us, she began screaming, "You filthy, irresponsible male! You had no right to take Victor for so long. Maybe fifteen or twenty minutes, but not forty. Your behavior was not appropriate. Not appropriate at all!"

Victor tried to say something.

"Go to your room, young man! Take the dog—*vite!*" Penelope ordered. "You'll get no dinner tonight."

He knew she meant business. He and Fifi were soon out of sight.

I looked at my watch. "We were gone for half an hour."

"Your behavior is highly inappropriate," Penelope said.

"You're repeating a term that we hear everywhere in therapy circles. Who the heck knows what *appropriate* really means, especially you?" I asked. I regained my composure. "You never gave us a time limit," I said "How were we supposed to know what you expected?"

"I don't have to answer such questions. You should have known better. I will not have people who act in an inappropriate manner around me, or my son. You should *never* have gone into his bedroom without a chaperone," she added, stringing her accusations together without taking a breath.

I said nothing, although I wondered how she expected me to know it was his bedroom. I'd never been to their home before.

Clearly, she expected everyone to read minds, hers at least. "You are unreliable and inappropriate. You should know better. You're supposed to be a therapist!" she screamed. "You should know whether something is inappropriate or not. You should know the importance of respecting boundaries."

By then, I knew that nothing I said or did was going to calm her down. Baltho had not sat down during her tirade.

He stood at my side. That clued me in on his read of the scene.

"You should never try to have friends. No wonder you don't have any," she yelled. "I want you to leave with your dog and never let me hear from you or see you again!" Penelope pointed to the street. "Now! Get walking."

"If you continue to be so controlling," I said, my volume and pitch low, "you will invite equal and opposite reactions from your son. Your reactions are over the top. You can't expect to control everyone and everything." Baltho had already turned and was pulling on his leash to go. I turned and began to walk away. Baltho certainly did not seem to be a dog who was falling apart that afternoon. Perhaps he was on the mend with the fall, as I'd hoped.

"How dare you talk back to me!" Penelope screeched. "How dare you! Out! I do not want someone who forecasts the future in my presence. I own my power as a woman who has the Lord! You are a fortuneteller and practitioner of witchcraft! I have nothing to do with idol worshippers and followers of false gods. In the name of Jesus, I order you—be gone!"

"I swear I hear a little growling," I said, laughing, walking, and looking down at Baltho, who kept glancing back a little menacingly, as if he were getting ready to fight another version of Tiny. "Careful. She's ready to stone us," I said. I stepped up my pace, for I could imagine the scenario too well. I recalled the scene from Monty Python's *Life of Brian,* where women dressed as men so they could stone the scapegoat. During that Biblical period, Judaism allowed only men to participate in public stonings. That many of the women in the Monty Python scene were men to begin with—playing women—playing men again—layered satire on irony on slapstick.

"To think that Penelope had once expressed an interest in dating me," I remarked, chuckling. "I tell you, Mr. Dog, I am so glad I saw the light. Praise God!" I shouted and hopped, lifting my hands to praise the Lord, with Baltho happily leading the way.

Webs

According to Penelope, I was a practitioner of witchcraft and a fortune teller. I didn't have to speak of visions and dreams to upset her. I saw more than she wanted me to see based on observation, education, and experience. Because my insights clashed with hers, I was of the devil, according to her.

I stood in my living room, with Baltho at my side. His head rested beneath my hand so that I could stroke him and know he was near. I recalled my earlier vision, where Baltho was standing beside me on a cliff's edge. The roiling sea seemed more threatening than ever, the dark clouds lower in the sky. I was brandishing my sword in warning, just as Baltho had taught me.

I wondered when the practice of stoning those who went against the vicious God of these militant, contemporary Christians would be put into practice. The way things were going, it wouldn't be long.

Penelope had stirred up my fears over religious extremes. The many divorces and remarriages among those who claimed to follow the Bible literally shocked me. St. Paul required that wives submit to their husbands, not kick them to the curb without good reason—and in a church service, no less. In fact, women in New Testament times were expected to submit themselves to men.

The doorbell rang. I went to answer.

A driver handed me a brown paper package. He reached to pet Baltho who had stuck his nose out in a friendly gesture.

I ripped off the wrapping. Inside were the sunglasses that I'd left at Penelope's house, along with a four and a half page, single-spaced, typed letter detailing all my faults. "You have no respect for boundaries. My boundaries are good. My therapists tell me that I have some of the best boundaries they've ever seen. I do not need anyone to forecast my future. I do not sit in the congregation with sinners. I do not entertain fortune tellers or practitioners of witchcraft and sorcery."

She ended with a number of lines telling me that Victor never wanted to see or hear of me again. "He told me I should not return your sunglasses but throw them away, or give them to the poor, if I couldn't bring myself to toss them in the garbage along with everything else related to you."

"Well Baltho, we know what they say about good deeds." I patted Baltho's head and reached for his Extenda Leash. He was ready for a walk, and I needed to put some distance between myself and the mental invasion carried out by Penelope.

"She must have experienced the John Gold brand of therapy," I told Mr. Dog, as we headed out, "the one where the therapist tells only a little of the truth, which can easily be construed as the hearer wishes. Of course, telling Penelope the truth and nothing but would invite some sort of grievance board inquiry and lawsuit."

That afternoon I drove to the office to pick up my mail. I rarely went in now, but saw most clients at home, where Baltho could help. Helen looked up from her desk. "Have you heard the news about Marty?" she asked.

"What?" My mind raced to the spot on the back of Marty's head.

"He's been diagnosed with liver cancer," Helen informed me. "That's why he's been feeling so rundown."

"What are his odds?" I asked.

"It's too early to know. "But it sounds as if things aren't good. He spent many years drinking and who knows what else." She looked around to see if anyone was near. "Gold is really running amuck, so be careful," she warned.

"Worse than usual?"

She nodded. "Yes."

"I think I'm leaving," I said. As I walked away, I knew I'd meant more than just going away from the office for the time being.

"I've had it," Helen told me when she phoned a few days later. "I've resigned. I haven't found another job, but things around there are going to get really bad," she said, "with Gold's cash supply taking a big hit. Marty brought in lots of clients, got the Golds lots of attention in the gay and lesbian community." We all knew Marty had the biggest clientele of anyone in the office.

Everyone was soon hearing rumors about Helen. "That Helen—she's such a bitch," Gold shouted across the reception area at me. I'd barely gotten in the door. Fortunately, no clients were present. Two part-time therapists, who wanted to get along with Gold, nodded slightly in agreement. "I'll fix it so she never gets another job again," Gold fumed.

Gold soon had a replacement for Helen, this time a young man named Lou. Gold referred to him as LouAnn. "Our gay clients will respond to him. He's hot."

Marty quickly deteriorated. He hardly came into the office. Gold told me that I ought to buy part of Marty's practice, since he had a huge number of clients. "I don't want to see us lose them." Twenty-eight client files, containing confidential information, soon appeared on my desk. On top of the pile was a list of the clients' names and telephone numbers.

I walked back to Gold's office. "These files make me uncomfortable," I said. "They're supposed to be confidential."

He was on the speaker phone. He hung up. "You worry too much," he said. "All information stays in this office, among Marty's colleagues."

"Is that what the law says?" I asked.

"I'm the ethics specialist," Gold responded.

Our new secretary, Lou, soon learned about Gold's superior knowledge in that area, so he dubbed him, "Mr. Unethical." But he didn't dare use that term to Gold's face. He needed his job.

"Fair is fair," I remarked, laughing.

Lou informed me that my colleague, Monica, also got a list of Marty's clients, "Along with their files. As far as I know, she hasn't been asked to pay for them. She's married to a Jew. Gold knows better. He doesn't want to enrage the Jewish community more than he already has. Becoming a Christian was bad enough."

When Gold, for my next supervision, hauled me over to Marty's apartment to talk about buying part of his practice, Marty quoted me a price of $26,000. "You can pay it in three installments over a year," Gold added.

I listened, nodded, and said, "I'll have to think about it." I hated to make Marty feel worse by saying what I really thought. I smelled another of Gold's schemes. I was willing to bet he was planning to take a percentage as a kickback.

I placed several calls to talk with clients on the list Gold had given me. I asked if they would like to see me. Most hemmed and hawed. A few set appointments but failed to show up. Several more saw me once or twice but didn't return. Obviously, I wasn't Marty. We were colleagues and friends. But his clients didn't want to see me. I'd heard he'd followed Gold's advice and listened sympathetically without offering much that could be construed as negative criticism. I wasn't that nice, although I tried to be kind about my criticisms.

"Taking Marty's clients isn't going to work," I told Gold as I caught him in the reception area. "I'm not comfortable with the entire process."

"Come back to my office," Gold said, taking me down the hall. He closed the door and told me that he'd heard me promise Marty that I would buy my portion of his client load. "I'll testify to that effect when Marty sues. My lawyer has promised to take the case."

"I am not going to be intimidated."

Gold put me on the line with his attorney. I said, "I've been mulling a plan. I don't want to be unfair to Marty, so I'll have my lawyer work out some sort of percentage for each of his clients who sees me." I paused, only half-listening to Gold's lawyer.

Emma must have sensed that her husband was experiencing distress. She slipped into the room.

"Emma, can you explain what your husband is up to?" I asked.

Emma shrugged. "I don't know a thing," she said.

I had always thought her to be the more honest and decent of the pair. With my jaw dropped, I continued to stare at her.

"I don't know of anything unethical in this office," Emma said. "We run an ethical practice. You even wrote a recommendation for John saying so. The HMOs have copies, I'm sure." She turned and walked away.

"That was before I got to know him so well," I called after her, the door whooshing shut behind her.

Gold stood. He grabbed my shoulders and turned me to face him directly. "If you don't keep your mouth shut, I'll pick up the phone, make a few phone calls, and destroy you. I don't mean just your practice." He paused. "I'd hate to do that. But it's the New Yorker in me."

Baltho flashed into my mind. No, I couldn't allow myself to worry that Gold would go after him too.

Gold sat down again and turned to the materials on his desk. He began shuffling papers. "You're dismissed," he said.

As soon as I got home, I contacted the lawyer that Lou had previously worked for. "He has an extra office in his suite," Lou had told me. "You could sublet that. Sharing an office suite with an attorney might help shield you from Gold."

I decided to move my office there. While Marty's health crisis had brought out the worst in Gold, the issues, or seeds of them, had been there all along. Over time, they'd grown and multiplied.

I talked with a number of people about reporting Gold to the State Regulatory Agency. Someone had to put a stop to Gold's abuse. Because he was after me, I figured I might as well be the one to head the effort. Baltho had shown me the necessity of standing up to Tiny, and this was one Tiny who wasn't going to terrorize everyone in the neighborhood much longer.

Helen said she wasn't sure that we should turn him in. "He's like a rabid dog, especially now. You don't know how he'll retaliate," she said. "And you can be sure he will."

"I'm getting defamed and threatened anyway," I said. "We have to be brave and do this."

Gold's good friend Bob had told me that he knew how to hex people. "You ought to learn how," Bob said. "I've taught John Gold and others. Your enemies can be kept at bay, their proper retribution guaranteed."

Before the therapy practice started falling apart, Gold had remarked, "People are scared of Bob. They go to his demonstrations of the black arts and leave because they're afraid of his powers." He paused. "I know I wouldn't want to cross him," Gold said.

I wondered what exactly Gold's motive in telling me this was. A warning that might prove valuable in future, it now seemed.

Finally, over an early December dinner at my home, Helen agreed that she too would come forward. "I'll speak of what I know of Gold's unseemly behaviors."

"Don't tell them how you had to stab his hand with your fork for daring to take another bite off your plate," I added. I nibbled at my green beans, slipping a couple to Baltho, who lay on the floor beside me. If Helen had noticed, she would have scolded me for feeding him from the table.

It took a moment for Helen to realize that I was teasing. "Too bad I didn't stab him elsewhere," she said, shaking her head. "He thought he'd keep you dependent forever."

Through my lawyer, I offered to pay twenty percent of all fees that I collected from any client that had been Marty's. Gold's attorney, now handling Marty's affairs, rejected the offer. Somewhere in the process, I found that selling one's clients, as well as client lists, was illegal.

Friends and I gathered the information, being as specific about names, facts and dates as we could. We ended up with an eighteen page, single-spaced complaint, which we turned in to the State. We expected the investigation to go on for at least six months, probably a year—or two. It would be quite involved, and Gold wouldn't go down easily.

The Dark of Time

In the bleak cold of February, Marty died. His death had come within a few months of diagnosis. I didn't attend his funeral. After the trouble over his client lists, I hadn't felt that I could even visit him.

I talked with Lou on the phone. "Gold loves to tell people how Marty looked like a monk at the end—old and wizened."

I didn't know what to say. "I can only wish Marty well on his new journey. We'd once been friends."

"Gold is now presenting spirituality workshops to seminaries and religious groups," Lou said. "He's claiming personal expertise in spiritual matters."

I could only shake my head in response.

Baltho now weighed eighty-four pounds. My weight had also steadily increased. I now weighed two-twenty, twenty-two pounds more than I had weighed at the time I'd adopted Mr. Dog. I attributed our weight gain to all the stress. We'd enjoyed peace for only short periods. Both of us had been getting plenty of exercise and eating well. I enjoyed lots of fruits and vegetables. Baltho liked all vegetables, especially carrots, potatoes, and beans. He also liked apples and pears, hand fed to him, slice by slice, just as I enjoyed them.

Baltho seldom wanted to walk for two, three, or four hours at a time, as we'd done our first years together. He seemed to max out at a thirty to forty minute walk at a good pace—along with a few meandering short walks marked by an energy burst. He just didn't have the stamina that he'd once had. I also felt easily drained.

I noticed Baltho's chest seemed to be getting thicker, especially on the right side, near the pit of his front leg. My own chest seemed to pooch out a bit more under the rib cage, but on the left instead of on the right. Mirror images of sorts. Perhaps because of some sort of muscular imbalance, my friend Marilyn suggested.

At the grocery store one day, I happened to run into Karen, a middle-aged nurse, whom I knew from the Cathedral. She had sponsored Gold for membership in the Episcopal Church. "I've been worried about you since I never see you at any church functions anymore," Karen said. She was always friendly and supportive. She tried to help everyone.

"I've tried to remain distant from everything regarding the Golds," I said.

"He's still being investigated," Karen said. "He's afraid he's going to get sued."

"By only one person?" I couldn't help the sarcasm.

"Evidently he and Emma left a client locked in the office all night. She couldn't get out."

I wondered what other deeds would be revealed over time.

A few days after seeing Karen, I was shopping again. I happened upon a new ring that caught my eye. The stone was of various shades of green, with striations of yellow. The mounting was silver with gold accents. I asked to look at it. I put the ring on, liking the way it looked and felt. The price was good.

I needed a boost, so I decided to treat myself. I handed the clerk my credit card and signed the slip.

I held my hand up to look at the ring again. The stone had split down the middle. I showed the jeweler, who drew back. She had an Eastern European accent of some sort, Hungarian was my guess. "Someone is trying to destroy you," she said, looking me over. "I've not seen that happen but once. In my youth, nearly forty years ago in Budapest."

John Gold hexing his enemies flashed in my mind. A cold chill came over me. I nodded.

"That man was dead within a week. So was his cat. Destroyed in a fire," she added.

"I guess I'm going to have to be careful to stay centered, meditate, and turn the Darkness back on the sender," I said, thinking of my strategy. My psychotherapy practice had been kicked in the teeth by the turmoil. It had never been large, but I'd made a decent living. Now it was miniscule.

"Remember to keep surrounding yourself with protection," the woman added. "I'll have the stone replaced free of charge."

When I picked up the redone ring, I found the new stone less attractive than the original. It was pale. It lacked the earlier one's color variations and depth. The ring was still attractive, and would have struck me as more so, had I not known what the first version, the one I'd paid for, had looked like.

A few nights later, Baltho was riding in the back seat of the car. I turned onto I-70 west. I pressed the accelerator, hitting 55 miles per hour. Within minutes, I heard a loud bang. Baltho let out a piercing yelp—I felt some sort of impact on the rear, right side of the car.

"Someone's shot at us!" I exclaimed. The threat of highway shootings in Los Angeles had been spreading to the rest of the country.

Spotting an exit, I turned off and slowed down, my heart pounding.

I listened carefully. The right rear tire had blown out. It was thumping. The car was steering hard. I managed to pull into the gutter, stop, get out, and look.

"Weird, these tires are less than a month old," I said. "They're Michelin top-of-the-line radials." Hardly a shred was left of the tread and sidewalls. I'd never before had a blowout. Only a few strings of rubber and the wheel remained.

I changed the tire, griming with grease and dirt my clothes and hands.

The next day, I hauled the almost bare rim into the tire shop. I handed the technician my receipt. He looked to see how new the tires were, then took a look at the rim. He remarked on how little of the tread was left. "There's not even enough to send in for testing." He hauled the rim outside into the daylight. "Usually, there's enough of the tire left to test for defects."

I asked if they'd had any other problems with these Michelins.

"No, they've been reliable. You're the first to return one—or what's left of it," he said. He was having a hard time wrapping his mind around the fact that this new Michelin had blown out. He kept looking at the rim, screwing up his face in puzzlement. He put the car up on the rack to examine the undercarriage with his light. He felt around with his hand. "I want to make sure nothing in the tire well or frame caused the damage."

"Thanks for being thorough."

"This," he concluded, "is very mysterious."

"Hello Mystery, my friend," I muttered, patting Baltho's head when I got back into my vehicle. He looked up at me. But he wasn't smiling.

Ringing the Bells

My former client, Darren, left a message on my answering machine. "Hey Tom, I just wanted to check in and let you know I'm doing well. My wife Brenda and I have adopted a dog from the rescue. He's a Golden Retriever mix, about four years old, a dog like I've always wanted. We think of him as our first child." He laughed. "The real thing is next in our plans."

I glanced over at Baltho, who was lying on the carpet, half asleep.

My neighbor, Jessie, laid into my front doorbell. She pushed again and hollered. "Hey Tom, I've been reading the Declarations and Covenants of this place." She wasn't one to keep her voice down.

Baltho managed to get up and follow me to the door.

"Have you read them?" she asked.

"No," I answered. "I wonder if anyone has."

"We could be in big trouble legally. Most of the rules aren't being followed." She began to walk inside. Her dog Sproing rushed in before her. He spotted Figgy and began chasing him around the house, upstairs and down—before Jessie grabbed the beast by the scruff of his neck and threw him out.

"Figgy, I don't know why you let Sproing terrorize you like that," I said. Baltho and I went over to him, cowering in the corner behind the couch. I picked him up to soothe him with my hand and voice. "And Baltho, why didn't you stop Sproing?" I asked. "I know the answer," I said, nodding. "It's okay. I know you just don't have it in you anymore."

"At least three times a day, just to show him who's boss, Sproing's own cat walks right up and swats him on the nose," Jesse said. "The cat hasn't been declawed, so he draws blood. Damned dog," she muttered. She took a seat at my dining room table, the legal documents that she'd brought with her in hand.

Still upset by Sproing's terrorism of Figgy, I said, "That probably explains it. Figgy is too nice. Figgy, you must think of Sproing as Tiny and you as Baltho."

"Here," Jessie said, handing me an extra copy of the Declarations and Covenants. "I figured you might not know where yours are."

I thanked her. I added, "I'm sure mine are in my filing cabinet."

"First of all," Jessie began, "we're required to have four officers, a president, a vice-president, a secretary, and a treasurer. We have two, right? A president and a treasurer, though Rita seems to have taken over everything."

I nodded. "Not surprising, is it? Mona is supposedly the treasurer, or is it the secretary?"

"Must be the secretary. The statements come from Rita. Technically, she shouldn't be doing a thing, since it's her husband, Ron, who was elected the chief officer."

"Let's see you budge her from that throne," I said.

"My husband has a gun or three," Jessie suggested. "We're from Texas. He hates everyone around here anyway."

I laughed, although I also felt an inner alarm sound.

"Now, look at this," she said, pointing out a paragraph in the Declarations. "This says the manager is supposed to be someone from outside the HOA. No officer is to be paid for his work."

"No pay, no work," I said. "That alone would make Rita resign."

"Since she doesn't love it, she gets paid, and since she can't get paid legally—that's it!" Jessie exclaimed. "She'll resign."

She and I typed up a formal grievance which we stuck in every homeowner's door the next day.

Suddenly, a handwritten message appeared in our mailboxes from Ron, saying that an urgent meeting was called for Saturday at 10:00 a.m. "All homeowners must be present," his note said.

When Jessie and I appeared in the common area, I glanced at Ron, who was fuming. I looked at Rita. She managed to appear under control, although I could tell from the set expression on her face that she too wasn't happy.

Right after the group began discussing the problems, Ron jumped up. He held his fists out at me. "I ought to pop you in the mouth for what you wrote about me," he said.

Two other homeowners, Twila and Jim, stood to flank Ron on both sides, ready to hold him back.

"Calm down," Rita said. "I don't trust people here anymore. Since Jessie and her family moved in, we've been taken over. Tom is always out in the back yard with his dog. So are Jessie's kids. The rest of us can't go outside and enjoy time by ourselves."

"I've heard the yard hasn't been used much for years, except by Tom, who as I've said, works in it every day," Jessie said. She chose to ignore Rita's comment about her family.

"That isn't true. Mona is often outside pulling weeds," Rita said.

"She is, now and then," I said. "I don't want to be unfair, but she isn't out working in the gardens nearly as much as I."

"Sonya has sometimes planted flowers," Rita added.

"That was some time ago," I said.

"Sonya sold her unit to me, remember," Jessie said, her voice growing sterner. "She rented it out before that. She hasn't lived here for years."

Quickly, we moved to a new item of business about yard cleanup. We decided to allow Jessie and me to head the taskforce. We were authorized to buy plants, fertilizer, pruning sheers, a shovel, rake, clippers, and the materials for a drip system, which I would install. We were given the green light to use Jessie's pickup to get recycled wood chips for free from one of the nearby county recycling plants.

"I just don't trust people here now," Rita repeated, unable to let go.

On Saturday evening, we got another note in our boxes. Ron resigned his office. Rita called a new election. A ballot was enclosed to be returned by Monday at noon.

"What's this?" I said to Jessie. "One of our complaints involved the elections. They're to be announced, with the results counted, within a window of ten to twenty days. Rita is giving people a little over a day."

"Think about it," Jessie said. "The votes from off-site can't be counted by then because they won't be able to get them in. We don't even know if they will be told about the election, and you know who'll win if only the owners living here vote."

I nodded. "Those hand-picked by Rita and Ron."

On Monday evening another handwritten note appeared in our mail boxes. "Congratulations to Mark, our new president, to Adolph, our new vice-president, and to Mona, our new secretary/treasurer. Adolph will be the new manager."

"Who the hell does this broad think she is?" Jessie fumed, appearing at my door right after I read the note.

"We did get a few changes."

"They're still not legal," Jessie said.

"I know I don't trust Adolph. I'd like to, but I've seen and heard too much about his habits," I said. I lifted my closed hand and guzzled air.

"As an owner of hotels and restaurants, I'm used to dealing with drunks," Jessie said. "One power broker resigns but makes damned sure others who take her place are easily controlled."

"Mark seems OK," I said.

"He seems intelligent," Jessie said. "Even though he's married, I'll eat my bippy if he isn't at least bisexual. If any of us shouldn't trust people here, it should be you and I."

By Memorial Day, Jessie and I had hauled in three pickup loads of free wood chips for the gardens. Some of the homeowners, including Mona, Adolph, and Mark—and even a few renters—picked up shovels and boxes and helped scoop them from the pickup. We spread them over the gardens.

I got a couple of people—both renters—to help me install the drip system in the flower beds. One was a business owner. "You've got to be careful of the Rivas," she said. "I knew Ron's first wife. She was a good woman." She paused, looking to see if anyone was around. "You know what Rita's like."

"I'm learning." I smiled wearily.

"I don't know why all these people still go to Ron for help. He and Rita never do anything without expecting a kickback of some kind."

Significantly, Ron and Rita never put in an appearance for any of our backyard improvements.

When we turned in the receipts to Mark, he said they should go to Rita. "She's handling them, since she was the one who authorized the expenditure."

So I hauled them to Rita. She opened her door, took them from me, and shut the door. Thirty minutes later, she phoned Jessie and me, telling us to meet her in the back yard, where she pitched a fit. "When I added these up, I saw they total $651. We aren't paying it. You shouldn't have spent so much."

"You didn't put a limit on us," Jessie argued. "You got a deal. Tom and I drove all around town wasting our time and our gas to find the best deals we could to make this a better place for everyone."

"We're going to have to take a vote. I can't authorize it," Rita said. She got Mark to call another meeting where she argued that the HOA should not reimburse Jessie and me. "Maybe we should pay half," she said.

"We can always rip things out and take them back," Jessie said, sarcastically.

"How much do you think you would have had to pay professionals to do this work?" I asked.

Finally, a vote was called. Jessie and I were reimbursed, with only Rita voting no.

A few days later, Jessie found a cache of receipts that she hadn't turned in. They amounted to nearly $300. "I'm not even going to try," she said, tossing them aside. "I really wish my husband would get drunk some night and make a house call or two."

The next night, I had another blow-out. Again, it was the right rear tire—the replacement. As before, I had been driving for a few minutes on the freeway and was going fifty-five to sixty miles per hour when it blew. It was mid-afternoon. I could spot no exit nearby, so I managed to steer the car out to the wide shoulder of the road and change the tire. I'd heard about people being hit doing just that, so it made me even more anxious.

Again Baltho was with me. As before, he let out a loud yelp on hearing the bang. The thumping and rough ride of a blow-out soon followed.

When I drove the car in to the tire shop, the repair man shook his head, and said, "I sure can't figure this out. I've never seen such total blow-outs. There's nothing left to test."

He replaced the tire, and I drove off.

When this happened a third time, again after hitting fifty-five miles per hour for a few minutes, the technician for the tire shop said, "Are you sure someone isn't attaching a detonation device to your tire? You said you park on the street, didn't you? Is that tire hidden by the curb and shrubbery?" he asked.

"Yes." My suspicions were gelling. "Yes, it would be the tire most hidden by the bushes at the curb."

"Your guardian angel must be watching over you," the man remarked. "We'll replace your tire for free again."

"Thank God for that," I said, glad for protection and that I wouldn't have to pay for a replacement.

"This time, there's a tiny shred of tread left. I'll send it in for testing."

I refused to be spooked by these occurrences. Even though the stone in my new ring hadn't cracked again, I'd felt psychic attacks on a regular basis. They often started subtly, as if I was being approached by heavy energy. Sometimes, I felt a black, dense cloud engulf me from the feet up, becoming thicker, like sewage sludge. When I became aware of it, I stopped whatever I was doing and focused on someone I visualized as the sender—it didn't matter who. I pictured a shield of white light emanating from within me and forcing the darkness away.

Then I gathered the bad energy into ball, multiplying its size and power by a hundred-fold. I rolled it back at the one who directed it my way. There, I watched it spread and engulf that person in darkness that became blacker and more palpable each time. They'd sent it. When they got it back, they received it in spades.

I talked with Helen about the blow-outs when she stopped by one afternoon. She complained of the heat and said, "I don't believe in hexes or curses. They're superstitious nonsense, like the warding signs that Episcopalians and Catholics make. That's what the sign of the cross is."

"You believe in the power of prayer, don't you?" I asked. Helen loved those positive spiritual books and gurus—as long as they weren't specifically Christian.

"Yes," she said.

"So why do you think that only good energy can affect our lives, but bad energy has no effect?" I asked. "I know you want to believe only in the good, yet your own life has constantly evidenced evil rushing in and threatening to obliterate you."

I had to run to answer the phone.

"I'll let myself out," Helen said.

I grabbed the receiver and answered. "You need to watch out," the tire man said. "The tests appear to confirm our suspicions. They indicate some kind of detonation device was planted on your tire. Traces of explosives were found," he said.

With the heat of summer starting, I kept the windows open. More and more often, Baltho got disturbed by a noise out in front of the building at night. He'd come to, jump up and run to the windows to bark—loudly, menacingly—at something, or someone, on the street below. Soon, he'd pushed the screen out so far that he could, with only a little effort, leap out the window and give chase. He would never survive a fall from that height.

Since my car was parked in front of my unit, I wondered if Baltho was threatening some thug that Gold had hired to sabotage my car. I just didn't know. When I got up to look, I couldn't see anyone. But I didn't have Baltho's keen sense of hearing.

I couldn't worry too much. I placed an old stainless steel oven rack up in front of the window to prevent Baltho from jumping through them.

We had to live—for as long as we were able.

Soon, I'd place the air conditioner unit in the bedroom window and close the door to sleep. Perhaps that would mask the noise coming from the street.

This Mortal Coil

Baltho and I completed the third month of our third year together. The summer had been hot, dry, and without any major incident. I'd had only a few phone calls from potential clients. I had even fewer actual clients.

My disgust with certain members of my profession certainly didn't help me remain upbeat about my career. Why, oh why, did I get involved with people who in truth cared nothing about others but only about advancing themselves and making money? It was a pattern.

Gold had at least made me laugh, even though he also disgusted me. I couldn't say that about either my former English Department Chairman or the Dean of the Cathedral. I wanted to think I was making progress, finding myself under the thumb of someone who was at least creative and fun, and not treacherous.

"Oh dog," I said, reaching to pet Baltho who lay at my side. "If I didn't have you to share my burdens and my joy, I don't know what I'd do. I know you're aging, but we'll keep going." I felt myself tearing up. "I don't want you to die. I want you to live a long life, even if you don't have lots of energy anymore," I blurted, unable to go on.

I stood, thinking I'd better grab Baltho's leash from the hook by the door. Going for a walk would get my mind off what seemed inevitable, although I didn't know how soon, or the manner of his death.

By September, Figgy had adopted a woman with two grown daughters across the street and down a few houses.

He started visiting there more and more frequently, and, before long, he didn't come home. They had several cats. Sproing's terrorizing him whenever he got the chance had encouraged him to find a new address.

"Figgy," I said, when he appeared from the back of the neighbor's yard one morning. He sauntered out to the sidewalk to greet me and Baltho on our walk. "Why didn't you throw yourself down and roll over onto your stomach when Sproing went after you the first time—as you did with Baltho? Once Sproing knew he had the upper hand, he kept on abusing you." I smiled sadly. "I suppose there's a lesson in it for me too."

Baltho sniffed at Figgy, who rubbed on his legs and on mine. Despite my coaxing, and Baltho's many pauses—as if to encourage Figgy to follow—Figgy wouldn't budge from his adopted yard.

Later in the day I hauled Figgy's twenty pound bag of dry Friskies and a twenty pound bag of cat litter over to the women's home. "We don't mind Figgy at all," the mother said. "One of our cats recently died, so we have room in our home and in our hearts. Figgy—Figaro, I guess it is—is a really sweet cat." She reached down to pet him.

"I know. You be careful, cat," I said. I bid him goodbye. Maybe all those cats and women reminded Figgy of my mom and sister Diane's homes.

While Figgy had retreated to what he knew best, the zone of greatest security, I had to push forward. If we don't grow, we wither and die. I had been increasing my knowledge of the complementary healing field, something in which I had long been interested. The use of alternative therapies, along with—but not in place of—regular Western medicine, seemed sensible to me, the best of all worlds. Ever curious, I wanted to observe various methods and modalities firsthand. Rather than take anyone's word, since people can be caught up in their need to believe, I would observe and conclude for myself what worked and what didn't.

I'd heard that I should check out Maria Lubshenka's spirituality center, located just outside of Idaho Springs. Having been run out of various municipalities for practicing medicine without a license, she built a large brick building just outside the city limits. Next to a motel, where people taking her classes could stay, her complex housed meeting rooms, a big kitchen, dining area, and a chapel. There, she continued her ostensibly Christian ministry, which centered on holistic health and teachings.

Lubshenka attracted a wide variety of healers and was well known as an herbalist and homeopathic healer. In long-ago youth she'd studied with a supposedly famous Russian, whose name rang no bells for me. She had an entire line of Lubshenka herbs. I'd heard they were of high quality.

Many people swore by her. Yet I worried that she and her entourage might be cultic. The alternative and complementary healing community was rife with people who were too far-out to be taken seriously. But then, all fields suffer from those who rise to the top, not through talent and knowledge, but through charisma and the regular application of hook and crook. These were more examples of Jesus' observation that, "The Kingdom of God hasn't yet come because the violent bear it away."

Various sorts of healers dropped into Lubshenka's—homeopaths, herbalists, aroma therapists, chiropractors, psychics, shamans, and the occasional African witch doctor. Then there was Lubshenka, a string-bean of a woman, with white, pinned-up hair and startling blue eyes.

She was only a little shorter than I. A spry woman of czarist certainty, she wore a sky-blue uniform with a navy-blue and white nurse's cap. On her breast she had pinned various medals. People saw their grandmother in her. She certainly wasn't anything like mine, who was afflicted by nervous uncertainty about everything. She would never have gone around telling people how they could solve their problems. She'd have helped them worry themselves to death.

One of Lubshenka's thirty volunteers introduced me to Lubshenka after her Sunday morning service.

"Oh good, I've prayed for a counselor to be brought to me," she exclaimed in her cheery, little old lady voice inflected with a Russian accent. Turning fierce, she added, "But don't make people cry. No one needs to cry. People must use their minds and be strong. We must help one another."

"OK," I said, knowing that tears can be therapeutic and iron wills can be dangerous. Helping one another to do better is good, but we can also help each into the darkness, to tumble down mountains and fall off cliffs.

"My dog is in the car," I said. "Could you have a look at him and see if you find anything wrong? He's slowing down.

One of the reasons I'd gone to Lubshenka's was to see if she or one of her followers could help him. Like a parent with a sense of growing desperation for his ailing child, I'd hoped for the opportunity to ask.

"On the right side of his chest, near the pit of his leg, some sort of tumor has been slowly growing," I said. "When I first discovered it several months ago, it was the size of a pigeon egg. I was petting him and noticed a lump that moved around as I felt it. It seemed just under the surface of his skin."

Lubshenka nodded.

"It's a lipoma, a fatty deposit," the vet told me. "Nothing to worry about. Dogs get them all the time. So do people. See how it moves when you touch it. Dangerous tumors are attached, hard. They don't move around."

Although I sensed a growing impatience, Lubshenka still nodded.

"It's now the size of a boiled egg—a chicken's egg, that is."

Lubshenka raised her hand. She'd heard enough. "Go get him," she ordered.

I walked down the long graveled drive to my car. Baltho was waiting. I opened the door and snapped on his leash. We walked back to the meeting hall in Lubshenka's complex.

She circled his body holding her quartz crystal pendulum on a sterling silver chain six inches above him. It continued to spin clockwise with a steady motion. "He's fine," she said. "There's nothing wrong. Don't worry."

I felt a little better. I hoped she was right, but the nagging premonitions of his doom still haunted me. I just didn't know what to do about that. What *could* I do? I knew I would continue seeking. Maybe someone who visited would be able to help.

Soon, I found myself doing some counseling after Lubshenka's Sunday morning church services. At that time various healers would practice their arts. Lubshenka was always present, with crowds lined up to have her diagnose their maladies, for which she had "just the solutions and rituals."

Being at Lubshenka's gave me a chance to practice my counseling skills and develop my intuitive knack. A good counselor needs both. And there I could definitely center on my spiritual ministry, which I recognized as my core.

Operating from one's spirituality, in my mind, is essential to health and wholeness.

Lubshenka used her pendulum over people's bodies as a way of diagnosing where they were having difficulties and appropriate solutions. Although people swore that she knew their problems and what to prescribe without having to use such toys, she offered courses to those who wished to learn to do the same. Anyone could use a pendulum and prescribe Lubshenka's herbs, which many followers did. Folks even mailed hairs from their heads so that she or her volunteers would pendle to diagnose and prescribe the proper herbs, long distance, for a donation of thirty-three dollars. (The herbs cost extra.)

One Sunday, her devotees gathered in the cafeteria of her main building to view her ability to look at photographs of people and know exactly their conditions and treatments.

After looking at one photo, and reading the letter that accompanied it, she laid a chart of the human body on a table beside the picture. "See," she said. She applied healing pressure to certain points on the chart with some sort of metal wand. "Healing energy is transmitted to the person represented by the chart. He'll soon be well." She looked around and smiled, her blue eyes beaming with certainty.

"Wonders never cease," I said. And so her followers believed. While open and interested in the paranormal, some of these practices struck me as farfetched, sometimes dangerous, even for my inquisitive mind—something right out of the Middle Ages or before. After all, I had also been trained to be skeptical and test things. If there was no scientific proof of results, the methodology had to be scrapped.

The following week, Nathan, a young man originally from Australia, showed up at one of Lubshenka's seminars.

He began to attend Sunday and weekday services. He was friendly and needed a place to stay while looking for work in the area. His parents now lived and worked in the States, and he too had a green card. Although he looked in his early twenties, he said, "I'm actually in my early thirties. Thirty-three, to be exact."

I talked with him several times, on separate occasions, before I told him he could stay in my guest bedroom for a couple of weeks while he looked for work. He had been sleeping in his van and the nights were getting cooler. They sometimes dropped below freezing.

I had met fellow travelers in Europe and roamed with them for awhile before we went our separate ways. I had even invited some to stop and stay with me when they visited Denver. My experiences had all been good, and I came away feeling enriched mentally and spiritually by my new associations, especially those with international experience. I was willing to take the chance on Nathan.

Nathan didn't care a whit that the veterinarian had said the lump on Baltho's chest was a lipoma. "If removed, it will only grow back," the vet had more than once assured me.

"Baltho reflects you," Nathan insisted. We were sitting in my living room on the winged-back chairs in front of the window. Baltho was sitting regally between us. "You've got to see in him what you should being seeing in yourself." So the tumor—now the size of small a Granny Smith apple just under the skin near the pit of his front right leg—according to Nathan, was a burden Baltho was carrying for me.

I hauled him in to see Dr. Smith again. "See how it moves when you push on it?" he said. "That's a fatty tumor. I've never come across one that's malignant."

"When will it stop growing?" I asked, still worried. "It's more than tripled in size over the summer. Suddenly it was the size of a chicken egg, but just as suddenly, it's blown up to this."

Dr. Smith shrugged and said it would stop. "I've never seen one get much bigger. I know you and this dog are bonded, but you mustn't worry so much," he said.

"You must examine yourself to see what burden Baltho is carrying, what he is trying to get you to come to grips with. What are you remaining blind to?" Nathan demanded one day, as we knelt on my carpet to examine the dog.

Baltho loved the attention and stood still, head high, while we looked.

I felt a huge load of guilt engulfing me when Nathan and I talked. I tried so hard to be self-aware and not act out of my Shadow side.

"The outer world is only a reflection of what we're projecting from inside," Nathan intoned. The notion had invaded New Age movements. Some Jungians believed that we attract outwardly what we are inwardly and seemed to push that notion to the max. I'd heard other strains of blame-the-victim talk in the past, when I'd traveled among charismatic Christians.

"I think such ideas are extreme," I said. But I promised Nathan I would earnestly consider them.

To my relief, Nathan suddenly decided to leave Denver. He'd used his pendulum over a map and decided that Alaska was the place for him. He'd find his fortune there. He'd stayed at my home for two months—at least four weeks longer than I'd wanted.

The trees outside were leafless. The weather was chilly but mild. We'd had little snow.

Fetching a cup of green tea, I sat in my chair in front of the living room window. Baltho lay beside me on the carpet, sleeping.

I had meditated for days on the notion that Baltho's hump, as I'd begun to think of it, was a literal reflection of my own spiritual hump. I'd searched to see if I could beat myself up over something—anything at all. I held the cup to my mouth and decided that animals do reflect us in some ways, but they also have lives, bodies, wills—and illnesses—of their own. To believe otherwise is to reject the sacredness of Creation, the notion that each living being has a soul—and individuality—of its own.

We must take responsibility. I wholeheartedly agreed with that notion. "But if God wants to teach me a lesson, I want him to teach me directly, not by making an animal suffer on my account," I said aloud. I reached down to rub Baltho's side. He was such a gorgeous, noble beast. How he'd come into my life I'd always regarded as a mystery, a glorious mystery from the heart of God.

"Mr. Dog, I think we've learned what we can at Lubshenka's," I said, pulling my sweater tightly around me. He raised his head, opened his eyes, and looked up at me. He opened his mouth and sighed. "Even Lubshenka didn't seem to think your lump was anything to be concerned about," I said.

I thought of the mad poet Christopher Smart. "He spoke of his cat, 'Jeoffry, who is the servant of the Living God, duly and daily serving him. For at the first glance of the glory of God in the East he worships in his way.' And so do you," I added, still looking at my compatriot.

Baltho stretched out, looked at me with his still-clear eyes, sighed contentedly, and went back to sleep.

Lines from Wordsworth's *Intimations of Immortality* came to mind. *This* was the remedy I needed:

Baltho, the Dog Who Owned a Man

Though nothing can bring back the hour
Of splendour in the grass,
Of glory in the flower,
We will grieve not, rather find
Strength in what remains behind;
In the primal sympathy
Which having been must ever be;
In the soothing thoughts that spring
Out of human suffering;
In the faith that looks through death,
In years that bring the philosophic mind.

Heart Talk

In late November, I gathered three healers—my psychic friend, Marilyn; Ron, an acupuncturist and Doctor of Oriental Medicine (O.M.D.); and myself. We would present what we termed the Heart Talk Café, a holistic workshop, in the Wild Oats Health Food Stores in Denver. We hoped to give people insights into their own issues in an entertaining way. We made certain to avoid saying or implying that we were giving medical advice. Any medical problem should be brought to the attention of the person's physician. Although we looked at people from our own particular framework, we found a remarkable amount of agreement on the health, mind, and soul issues facing each participant.

"I don't think it's a good idea to be too predictive. We need to stay with what appears to be going on in the person's life here and now," I instructed them. "Dipping into the past to discover the present is reasonable," I added. "If we see patterns that are likely to influence the future, that too is okay. But we have to avoid the trap of fortune telling. In other words, let's stay away from predicting a tall, dark, handsome stranger, who'll sweep in and marry you in six months."

Marilyn knew that I was speaking especially to her. She laughed and nodded.

I thought I'd better explain my reasoning. "Predictions like this tend to make people rely on what someone tells them is going to happen, rather than paying attention to the choices they need to make. Everyone needs to be involved in their own lives—that is, to practice the art of presence."

"You're saying we don't use our heads," Marilyn teased.

"Presence is more than just using our heads," I said. "It centers in the heart and involves our whole being."

"No one needs more fragmenting," Marilyn said, a subject with which she was intimately acquainted.

"As long as you go over well, we'll continue," said Clarice, the manager of the Wild Oats Market in Cherry Creek. They were interested in hosting our workshops twice a month. I placed ads in a couple of local newspapers and put out fliers at various coffee shops and holistic markets around town, especially in central Denver.

At our first event, we enjoyed a nice crowd of eighteen people. The room Clarice had assigned us upstairs—"our usual workshop space"—wasn't large enough to hold everyone who showed up for our second session.

"We don't have enough room to expand the circle," I said, going downstairs to find Clarice. It was six-thirty. We needed more space.

"Believe me, we don't mind. You're bringing in customers," she said, opening a large room used for storage. We moved boxes to the sides and got all participants to help haul in the chairs from the other room, plus others we managed to round up from various areas. We formed a bigger circle.

"I hope we bring in clients for ourselves," I said to myself.

When we settled, people introduced themselves. We had about two women for every man.

"Who would like to stand in the center of the circle and have us tell you what we perceive?" I asked. "Remember, we're not trying to take the place of your medical doctor, whom you should see if you have medical issues."

One well-dressed woman with white hair stood. "I'm Mary."

With his O.M.D. training, Ron checked her pulses and examined her tongue. Using her psychic sense, Marilyn gazed at her. I moved my consciousness slightly to the side and scanned her body, opening my spiritual perception.

Since I was the leader, I went first. I said I perceived some kind of irritation or block in her heart chakra. "I think it's spiritual, probably from a loss."

"Your pulses and tongue show some circulation issues," Ron said.

"You recently lost your husband," Marilyn said.

Mary, who had remained still, nodded. She began to weep softly. When she could speak, she said she'd been trying to work on her grief since her husband of forty years had died of a sudden heart attack. "He was walking in Washington Park. I wasn't even with him. That day, I couldn't go."

"You mustn't blame yourself," Marilyn said. "If you relax and trust, you'll find that he often visits to make sure you're all right,"

The night went on like that. When I looked at my watch, I saw it was nine-fifteen. "We have to stop. We're way past time."

"Can we come again next week?" an older woman asked.

I laughed. "I wouldn't come next week. The next Heart Talk is in two weeks. But yes, you're welcome to keep coming. I expect every workshop to be different because peoples' needs vary."

The second time we had twenty people. People began introducing themselves.

I kept being drawn to a woman sitting directly across from me. I wasn't sure why. She had beautiful green eyes and a nice smile. I began to perceive some kind of large iguana attached to her right arm.

When it was her term to introduce herself, she said, "I'm Jolene. I just returned from Machu Piccu."

"I'll bet you had a great time," Marilyn said.

Jolene nodded. "The scenery was spectacular and the people were some of the best I've ever traveled with."

"Your pulses and tongue look pretty good," Ron said. "That's rare, but it sometimes happens."

"I keep sensing that you've brought back something with you in the spirit realm," I finally said. "It seems like a big iguana or something like that. I don't sense that it's anything bad but just attached to you for some reason."

Jolene's eyes brightened. She nodded. "I've been having strange dreams since my last night there. I keep thinking a lizard is crawling on me."

"I think you can just tell it to leave you, and it will," Marilyn suggested.

Jolene said, "Please leave me," and it disappeared.

One of the men, maybe in his thirties, stood to have us look at him. He seemed very uncomfortable in the suit and tie he was wearing. "I'm John. I'm an attorney."

"Oh good," I joked, "you'll sue us if you don't like us."

He blushed.

"I didn't mean to embarrass you," I said.

"People always worry I'm going to sue them. I can't find real friends, at least not the kind I want."

Rather than go to his relationship issues, which seemed obvious, I noticed that he seemed to have some sort of blockage in the second, genital, chakra that marks creativity and procreation. Both stem from the same source.

"You know, John," I said, "I think you're a frustrated artist of some sort. You need to express your creativity."

"Or have some kids," Marilyn said, straight-faced. She grinned. "I was joking."

"Your pulses indicate you've got some allergy problems," Ron said.

John nodded. "That's true."

"If you weren't frustrated," Marilyn said, "your allergies would be better."

I returned to my central observation. "I still think you need to find a way to use your creativity. Allow yourself—make the time—to create."

John nodded. "I've always wanted to be a writer. But my dad said it was too risky and dubious a profession. He's an attorney. I needed something safe. He pressured me to carry on the family tradition."

"Only you can figure out what you need," I said.

Marilyn agreed. "Being safe just isn't you. You need to create, as Tom said."

Marilyn said later that she figured I'd get John as a counseling client. "He could use help sorting things out. He needs to write."

I never heard from John. It was becoming more evident that people preferred healers who worked on their bodies to those who centered on their psyches. This was similar to my experiences at Lubshenka's. People wanted herbs and rituals. Those were easier than delving into their innermost recesses and prodding them to work on their psychological and spiritual issues.

"Once again, my attempt to enlarge our client base is failing," I told Baltho one night when I got home from the Heart Talk. I grabbed his leash and took him to the door.

When I looked down at the entry way floor, I realized that someone had stuck a note under my door. "I've sold my house and will be moving on the 21st, Jessie." That was only three weeks away. "We'll be home in Texas for Christmas."

"I didn't even know you had this house up for sale," I told her the next morning, when I'd walked over to see what was up.

She invited me into the kitchen for a cup of coffee. "I don't feel safe here," she said. The people who control this Homeowners' Association operate outside the law. I wouldn't put anything past them."

"I hope it isn't that bad," I said, "but, gee, what do I know." The thought sent chills up my spine, although it didn't shock or surprise me.

"I put in all this work to make the place elegant—another bathroom upstairs, hard wood floors throughout, and we can't stay. We have to go back to our house in Dallas." She shrugged. "Another adventure. That's what life is made of." She laughed.

I wished Jessie and her family well. I wondered what things would be like without her around to help deflect the wrath.

Unless Adolph let the water pipes burst in front of my unit because he once again failed to have the irrigation system blown out, things might remain fairly calm. "In fact, with Jessie gone, maybe Rita and Adolph will lighten up a little," I told Baltho when I got back inside my unit. He was lying on the floor in front of the couch. I knelt down and petted him. His hair was so soft and thick. I stroked his head, noting again how it framed his handsome face. He looked at me. Our connection was still strong.

He groaned, a deep, comforted noise, and stretched. "I wish I knew what to do for you. I so want to believe you'll do better." I searched for something positive to tell him. "We won't have Sproing running into our house anymore.

Maybe Figgy will come home. I know you liked his company." I recalled their first meeting, how Baltho rushed over in a fit, but Figgy rolled over, disarming Baltho, so they became friends.

Slowly I got up, as if feeling the burdens of the world in my bones. I looked out the window. Winter was setting in. I knew I'd have to pressure Adolph to get him to see that the irrigation system was blown out before the heavy freezes set in.

"For someone who's paid to manage the place, he certainly does a rotten job. I know, he doesn't love it," I said, laughing to myself.

The winter proved uneventful. My new next door neighbor, a single woman, kept to herself. She had a cat that stayed inside all the time.

I continued to try our Heart Talk Café in other Wild Oats venues during alternate weeks. None worked so well as the Cherry Creek location. They were glad to keep us twice a month, so we stayed.

Basically, I still was volunteering, the story of my life. "Boy oh boy," I said to Baltho one day as I sat on the floor beside him and brushed his hair. "We've got to figure out a way to make some money." I pulled the hair away from his face. His eyes hadn't clouded with age.

"Well, keep trying," I imagined him saying.

"I know you know a lot about trudging on, no matter what, but I'm not sure you know much about money," I said, sadly smiling. I recalled those first days when I thought how much he'd like to live under a bridge and forage for food as we found it. The thought used to be whimsy. But now, with the chill and barrenness of winter coming on, it took on a grimness it'd never had before. I shuddered. "That might still happen."

Hump

With March, spring, like Persephone, arrived again. Crocuses and snow drops were followed by daffodils and tulips. Even though the days were sunny, a damp chill hung in the air. The double-brick firewalls of my townhome would hold the cool long after winter had gone.

I stood in the shower, water off. I was soaping up. I had to hurry because I never had the thermostat higher than sixty-eight degrees, even during the day. I set it at sixty overnight. The bathroom was huge. Even with the door shut, the room was cold.

In my mind's eye, Emma Gold stood in the midst of a large grassy field. A great foot appeared from nowhere and kicked under her groin. Like a football, she sailed through the air and landed a football field away. Lying on the grass, she looked like a rag doll.

Shivering, I turned the water back on and rinsed off.

I saw John Gold inflating like a huge balloon, getting bigger with every puff. He was so full of air that he could barely touch the ground. He bounced up and down. Then, with a final bounce, higher than before, he burst—then shot down like a dirigible that had caught fire.

With a heavy heart, I got out and dried off. This was no daydream. It was too strong to be that. It was a vision. In my experience, such truths, expressed in symbolic forms, always came to pass, rarely literally, but in their essence. I didn't know when these events would manifest. Gold's inflating bigger and bigger was already in progress. But I had to ponder the vision of Emma. What did it mean? It was harder to decipher than the vision involving her husband.

In a year, Baltho's tumor had grown to reach from his chest into his armpit. It was the size of a stale grapefruit. Rather flattened, but heavy, it hindered his mobility. He had trouble climbing stairs, especially the steep steps going in and out of my front and back doors. Even though the steps were limited to six, and necessary to get into the house, Baltho had a hard time managing them. He would stand at the bottom of the steps, staring—trying to gain courage. Finally he'd try his front right leg, but then stop, back up, and try to lead with his front left leg—then retreat—then start all over, as if the pain was too great to force his way through.

Most of the time, I lifted the front half of his body up, so that all he had to do was pull his back legs up, and go in the door. If he hadn't been so long, so heavy, and so awkward, I could have lifted his whole body and helped him. When he walked, he looked off-center. He had to swing his right leg out around the tumor in order to move.

Sometimes now, he even stayed downstairs when I was in my study upstairs or in bed. Those stairs however were easier than the outside ones. They weren't as high, but there were many more.

Baltho's limited mobility meant he no longer tried to get up onto the bed, even though I tried leaning a plywood sheet against the end of the mattresses so that he could use it like a ramp from the carpet. "At least you aren't in a wheelchair," I said, making a lame joke. "It would never fit in this area." I tried to get him to walk up the ramp. But he wouldn't. He didn't feel steady enough on his feet. "I'm sorry. You don't have to keep trying," I said. "Maybe later."

I recalled the past with sorrow. He had rarely slept with me during the entire night, not unless it was very cold outside, the kind of cold that invaded the old brick walls and ill-fitting windows of my townhome. Then I'd feel this *whomp* as he'd hit the bed—or more often, land on me, especially on my leg or sometimes my stomach or side—only to become restless an hour later, when he got hot and found that he wanted more room. Before deciding to jump off, he usually turned perpendicular to me, his head facing outward. Then he would start pushing with his long hind legs, so that he soon had much of the bed, while I was crowded to the edge. As I've said, he pushed hard. If he got cold again, he'd jump back up and we'd go through the same routine.

For some reason, nap-time had always been different. Perhaps Baltho saw that as a game, a sort of doggie kindergarten nap-time activity, much more fun than the nighttime routine. Whenever I'd lie down for a nap, no matter how hot the weather, he'd jump up, stretch out alongside me, his body next to mine, and stay that way. I'd put my arm out to pet him, noticing again the softest, thickest hair that I'd ever felt, and he'd wrap his arm around my arm, tangling our limbs together. Sometimes he would put his paw into my hand so that I could feel his webbed toes and knuckles, and massage the pads underneath. Then, he would switch to the other paw so that we could repeat it. When he tired of the attention, he would fall asleep with his nose tucked inside my hand or on my chest. Soon I too would sleep, one of us stirring an hour later to wake the other one.

On Monday of Easter week, I woke from a nap to find Baltho lying on the floor beside the bed. I rolled over so I could reach him. As I gently stroked the hair of his head, sliding down his side, I shook my head. "I'd hoped you might try the ramp for naptime. But you never have." I winced, trying not to tune too much into his pain. "It must be awful. I miss having you sleep at my side," I said, patting his side.

"I hate to think what you're going through." Knowing how difficult life had become for him made me shake my head in consternation. I took another look at him and recalled how hard it was to move. We ate sorrow like bread.

I decided to coax him downstairs with me. He needed to go outside and go to the bathroom. I knew he also needed a little exercise.

He lumbered to the front door. I took his leash from the hook by the door and attached it to his collar. Slowly, he made his way out and down the steps.

I knew that I had to get him to the vet. He was suffering too much to let things go any longer. I was also in agony for him. I coaxed him to the car parked in front. Every step hurt him, although he never cried. Baltho stood patiently beside the back seat waiting for my help. He didn't try to jump up, as he once would have done.

I bent down and hoisted his front half with my hands under his midsection so that I didn't cause more pain. He was able to position his front legs on the back seat without yelping. When I lifted his rear end, he managed to move his front legs enough to get his back legs and tail safely inside. We drove to the vet, ten minutes away.

When we got inside the examination room, I said to Dr. Smith, "You have to remove Baltho's tumor. We can't wait any longer. I know you don't want to remove it, but Baltho's quality of life has deteriorated because of it. So has mine. He can hardly go on walks anymore, even short ones."

I turned to Baltho, whose head was under my hand. "I'm sorry, Mr. Dog. I know we've got to do something about this." I'd said it so many times already.

Dr. Smith finally agreed. He had an opening to perform surgery at the end of the week, on Good Friday. I was to have Baltho there at eight a.m. "See that he has no food or water after six on Thursday," Dr. Smith ordered.

Maundy Thursday and the darkest spiritual night of the year, followed by the Friday that Christians call *Good* because of the hope that rises from the crucifixion. Perhaps this year, Baltho and I would experience an Easter resurrection, following the dark days of Easter Week, which, for us had lasted more than a year.

On Friday, I had Baltho at the vet's office by eight. At the back of my mind, I harbored fears that he wouldn't come through the anesthesia. I went home, waited and prayed—and paced—while he was in surgery. Like him, I had to be a good trouper. I took things in faith. At noon I phoned the vet.

"Baltho has come through just fine," Dr. Smith's receptionist, Kathy, said. "He's groggy but awake. I'll let Dr. Smith talk to you."

"You don't need to leave him here overnight," Dr. Smith said. "I've never seen such a large lipoma. It weighed almost four pounds. But it's benign," he assured me.

"Are you sure?" I asked, biting my lip. I remembered too well those forebodings of doom that I'd experienced so many times.

"I'm sure," Dr. Smith said. "You can come pick him up. Baltho's a real trooper."

I asked about pain medication.

"He doesn't seem to be suffering a lot," Dr. Smith said. "I don't think he needs anything."

I'm sure the shock of that statement registered on my face.

"If he starts acting like he's in a lot of pain, give him a Tylenol," Dr. Smith said.

Even with a number of stitches that marked his chest like a long zipper, with four long drain tubes descending from the stitches, Baltho tried to jump up into the back seat on his own. "Wait!" I insisted on helping him. "We can't let you rip your stitches open. I know you're brave and strong and true, but let me help till you're mended."

Until the drain tubes were removed in a week or so, depending upon discharge, Baltho would have to stay in the kitchen downstairs. I had to take care not to let him stretch his legs too far and pop his stitches.

He seemed to understand that he had to stay in the kitchen for awhile. When I left the room to go upstairs, he would look at me but not insist on following. Even at night, Mr. Dog didn't cry out or leave the kitchen.

The next day, I had to leave him unattended for a few hours. I had to meet with some fellow therapists who had attended the same training program as I.

When I returned, I noticed a huge puddle just inside the kitchen doorway. Baltho's stainless steel mixing bowl of water was empty. He must have drunk a couple of quarts. No wonder he couldn't hold his pee. I knelt to pet him and look at his wound. It was healing nicely. "Rapidly," I exclaimed. I hugged him, careful not to disturb the stitches.

"Your immune system is strong. Soon, you'll be ready for some long walks again," I said. "And able," popped into my head. I laughed, wondering whether Baltho was suggesting that, or if it had just come to me. But he seemed to pull his lips back into a slight smile and nod. He was such a good dog. He acted more like his old self all the time. I hoped for a full recovery. I could imagine us bounding through lower downtown and up toward the Capitol again.

Later that evening, I opened the refrigerator to take out some leftover baked chicken for dinner. I had cooked it the day before, only eating a leg and thigh, giving Baltho the liver, heart, and gizzard—which I chopped and mixed into his dry dog food.

I pulled out the uncovered baking dish and saw that it was completely empty—except some browned grease left along the sides.

Baltho was standing beside me, his nose poking at the containers. It seemed as if he was searching for something good to eat— "Something else, that is," I remarked, with mock scolding. I reached down to put my arms around his shoulders and my head on his head.

"I guess that clears up the mystery of why you were so thirsty. Too much salt perhaps. Too much chicken," I said. "And bones," I added. "All we need is for you to choke to death, now that you're on the mend."

How could I be angry? Baltho was helping himself to lunch. He deserved some comfort. But I did hope that some bones didn't splinter on the way through his system.

Two days later, I returned from some errands. Again, I noticed the refrigerator door standing an inch open.

I glanced inside to see what Baltho had eaten. I saw nothing. I hadn't put any meat in the refrigeration compartment. I closed the door.

By then, Baltho stood beside me. "I guess you didn't find anything to your liking." I shook my head, though rather amused.

When we walked back to the living room, I realized that I'd been wrong. There on the emerald carpet, on the other side of the dining room table, was an overturned quart of Mile High plain, non-fat yogurt. The lid was missing. Most of the contents had been licked out. A little had spilled onto the carpet.

"Well, you've learned a new trick," I said, more amused than disturbed.

When I returned to find the refrigerator opened again the day after that, I was really glad that Baltho was scheduled to have his drain tubes and stitches removed in a day. Feeling more whole, less needful of special privileges, he would perhaps forget his new trick, and go back to leaving the refrigerator alone.

To help Baltho recover more quickly, I took him to Jane, a friend who did massage, touch therapy, and energy balancing work. I'd found that her treatments made me feel better, so I asked if she would also work on him. She ran her hands over his body to scan for energy blockages, which she released by holding various pressure points on his legs and back. Then she massaged his hips, especially the back ones.

"Try adding some fish oil capsules to his food," she suggested. "It isn't toxic and helps lubricate the joints."

Like me, Baltho seemed to perk up. He got around more easily, with fewer moans.

I had been giving him glucosamine-chondroitin capsules since he'd started slowing down because the vet had thought he was getting arthritic. When he first started the glucosamine-chondroitin, it seemed to help. Then the tumor blew up and set things back.

As soon as Baltho had fully recovered from the operation to remove his tumor, the vet suggested I try giving him Rimadyl for arthritis. That also seemed to help. "It's an anti-inflammatory, but possible side effects are liver and kidney failure," Dr. Smith warned. "I know you like holistic medicine, but I don't think you should be experimenting with herbs on him, since we didn't know how they might react with the Rimadyl or Baltho's chemistry. Dogs' physiology is close to humans' but not quite the same," he said.

Baltho and I were able to start walking again. We began to saunter down the block and back, placing one foot in front of the other, one step at a time. He led with his right leg again. I felt like a physical therapist. By the end of the week, we were able to walk down the block and around it.

"Do you want to try a little further?" I asked, at the end of the third week.

Instead of turning to go around the block, Baltho had walked forward to the curb. He was trying to step off and go further.

"OK, let's go on," I said. "But you mustn't push too hard."

He slowly led across the street, with me at his side.

Soon, we could make it around two blocks, then three—and sometimes, when things went well, four blocks. I didn't dare push him any further than he signaled. I always let him take the lead.

The neighborhood kids would spot him and run to hug him." Why does he walk like an old man?" one little boy of maybe eight asked. His question was not unusual.

"He's getting older," I answered. I watched as he and his friends patted and hugged Baltho. He no longer perked up and clowned for anyone. He stood still and accepted the affection.

Three of the taller boys reminded Baltho how they found him. "We brought you home, full of stickers and mud," they said.

"Oh, you were the boys," I said, trying to recall their names—"Tony, Jose, and," I paused, "Juan," I said.

They nodded. "You've got a great memory!" Tony said.

I realized how fast they were growing. "Do you guys know it's been four years now since Baltho came to live with me?" I asked. "I used to recognize you, but I've lost track of the changes. I'm glad to know you're still good kids. Someone—rather, many folks—are doing the right things. Ours is a neighborhood."

Tony bent to kiss Baltho's forehead, just as he had the first time he'd met him.

Juan followed by bowing.

"Balthazar, you are still a noble king," said Jose. He genuflected like a gaunt knight and then kissed Baltho's nose and hugged him.

I had to wipe my tears with my sleeve. Baltho and I walked away.

In order to take longer walks for myself, I would take Baltho back to the house, pat him goodbye, and tell him guiltily that I would soon return. Then I would walk quietly to the door, close and lock it, and go off on my own. I had to get more exercise than just walking four blocks could provide. I hoped Baltho understood.

When I first started appearing without Mr. Dog, the neighborhood kids would come out to ask where he was, their faces registering anxiety. I told them, "He still isn't doing very well," so they'd tell me, "Give him extra hugs for us." Some said they'd say the Our Father for him, others promised the Rosary. "The Blessed Mother always hears the prayers of her children," said Jose.

"St. Francis keeps him under his wings," a little girl, wearing a white frock, as if dressed for her first communion, remarked one day. I'd never seen her before. I hardly ever saw girls on our walks through the neighborhood, almost exclusively boys. I wondered who she was. She'd come from nowhere. Why wasn't she with her family?

Finally the kids stopped asking. They glanced up to see me walking by myself. I smiled. They smiled. But then they'd turn and go on with their play, as if afraid to inquire.

One day, one of the neighborhood women approached me from her yard. She looked to the right, and to the left, to see if anyone was near. No one was within hearing distance. "I think your name is Tom."

I nodded. "Yes."

"You don't know me, but I've heard about Balthazar, or Baltho, from the kids. Everybody's heard of him," she said. "The kids love him. They always talk about him as the defender of the poor and weak. He scared Tiny into laying off them for good."

I smiled. I couldn't say much. I felt that I was going to cry.

"You can't imagine how disturbed they are now that he's so sick," the woman said. Her eyes darted away from me to see if we were still alone.

"I'm from Texas. There, people who want to get rid of animals by taking revenge on them and their owners give them small doses of a poison they get in Mexico. They lace meat with it and slip it to the animal," she said. She paused, looking around us again. "Your dog eats whatever he finds in the yard, doesn't he?"

I felt my fear of Gold's taking revenge on Baltho rise from the pit of my stomach. I swallowed and tried to press it down. "Yes," I replied, "if he gets the chance. Rather, he used to. He liked to eat what the squirrels hauled out of the garbage bin outside the gate and dropped as they scurried across the top of the fence." I paused. "He's rarely out on his own now. I don't think he's eaten anything other than the food I give him for months."

"Assassins adjust the dose so the dog will die quick or over the course of months, even years. It causes the internal organs to break down. That way, they control how much pain they give the owner and the dog." The woman paused, waiting for the information to sink in.

Helen had told me the story of a neighbor who poisoned the family dog when her boys were small. To me, such behavior seemed next to unimaginable. But I knew those possessed by evil were capable of anything. I wouldn't know if the food Baltho had eaten outside was dropped by the squirrels or if it had been slipped to him by some malignant soul. The damage could have been started years before.

"This poison is outlawed in the United States, but people can easily get it in Mexico," the woman said. I thought of those in the townhomes who wanted to run things, spring-boarding from the Homeowners' Association into the world at large. Rita had gloated over the fact that her minions had won the election called after her husband's abrupt resignation. My later complaints about Adolph's incompetence and neglect had gone ignored, proving that we could go from bad to worse. These people certainly had Mexican connections.

Thoughts of the Golds surfaced again. I thanked the woman and said goodbye. I needed to get back to the house. The Golds visited Mexico on a regular basis. They'd spoken of buying another home there. John Gold had vowed to destroy me, not just my practice.

I felt like vomiting. I stumbled on uneven sidewalk and almost fell face down. Gathering my courage, I walked on.

Gold might have decided to go after my dog—along with the hexes and detonations of my tires.

My head spun with the possibilities, all of them grim. I didn't want to believe the worst. If a poisoner had targeted Baltho, I might not have noticed. Feeding him poison would only have taken a moment.

The warnings had alerted me to possibilities. Still, I didn't know how credible they were.

I had been thinking that I should close my office and work out of my home alone. That way, I could cut expenses further. Clients didn't mind seeing me there, and I could be with Baltho constantly.

As I turned the corner and saw my townhome door, I decided to notify the lawyer from whom I sublet office space of my decision. I wondered if Baltho would notice my return.

Reading the Signs

One early evening in May, Baltho and I passed my neighbors' male Bearded Collie, Boomer. He was snooping around at the far end of Mike and Sean's yard, a block from my townhome. Baltho and Boomer were old friends. Boomer sniffed and seemed determined to pee on all the flowers that he could manage. Baltho saw him and made his way from the sidewalk over to the white picket fence. Boomer scampered over.

Both of them began to engage in their old peeing contest. Baltho would pee on the outside of the fence, and Boomer would follow by peeing on the inside just opposite him. Boom Boom, as I liked to call Boomer, would follow each pee of his own with a little dance made by kicking his back legs in the air and moving backwards with each kick. Baltho then had time to move a few feet from where he'd first peed and lift his leg again, with Boom Boom scurrying to catch up. Then he'd pee and kick his heels as he danced backwards.

Their act never ceased to amuse viewers. Mike and Sean, Boomer's human companions, and I often wondered aloud just what it meant. It didn't seem some sort of dominance ritual on either part. We wondered if it weren't some sort of "getting to know you" rite.

Maybe our trying to put such signs into words that we humans could understand wasn't always wise, because the ritual seemed to exist somewhere outside our understanding. We could only get a glimpse of their meaning. Regardless, I was glad to see Baltho regaining more of his old self.

As Baltho and I made our way home, the light of day dimming, I pondered these themes. I wondered how the Heart Talk Café that I'd thought up and headed was going to fare without our acupuncturist and O.M.D., Ron, who was moving to Hawaii.

I had to find a suitable replacement. Ron, Marilyn, and I had worked well together, with no one hogging the spotlight. Finding a third person who meshed well with Marilyn and me wasn't going to be easy.

Standing at the front door of my townhome were Ann and her Labrador Retriever, Choc.

"We were about to leave," Ann said.

I invited them in. Ann would provide a good sounding board for my latest ruminations. "Hey," I began. "I recently read of Colorado State University professor Temple Grandin's work with livestock. She has high functioning autism and says that animals think in pictures. She argues that rough handling or poorly designed equipment frightens them because they see what appear as dead ends. This is detrimental to both animal welfare and meat quality. It's also inhumane."

"I know you're trying to illuminate things with your words, but alone they won't do, not in all this darkness," Ann said, staying in the foyer. "I don't know if I'm heading into a dead end or the abyss."

Laughing, I went to turn on some lights. "Sorry. Let there be light."

"You've still got lots of the absent-minded professor about you," she said.

"I think it's more correctly the preoccupied professor. That's different from absent-minded."

"Thank God somebody is doing something about the practices of the meat industry," Ann said. "I'm so glad I'm a vegetarian." She glanced at Choc, who was busy sniffing Baltho's entire body, starting at the rump, while Baltho sniffed his body in return.

"I wonder whether animals translate such pictures into some rudimentary language, or if they leave things as pictograms. If animals are able to think without translating things into words, we human animals might be able to do so too."

"I jump when something I see scares me," Ann said. "I don't translate the situation into words before I act."

"But you do afterwards, right?"

She nodded. "Maybe my initial response is automatic, a reaction designed to preserve life." She petted Choc. "I believe Choc thinks," she said. "I just wish I knew what. Of course, I sometimes think I know."

I nodded. "I understand. Do animals later translate pictures into words, or do they stop with images?" I asked. I offered Ann a glass of wine and told her have a seat on the couch. In the kitchen, I poured and then brought back two glasses of Beaujolais. It wasn't French. It was Berringer of California, which would be just fine with Ann. Ann had been trained in English, as I had, although she hadn't gone on for the Ph.D.

"As you know, many moderns are saying that signs can mean whatever we want them to," I said, handing Ann her glass. I sat at the other end of the couch and wondered how long it would be before both dogs decided to join us on the couch.

"Tell that to me when I see some thug with a knife coming at me," Ann said.

Baltho, the Dog Who Owned a Man 217

"Context influences our reading, but it isn't everything," I said. "It's a guide. The larger patterns inform our general habits of interpretation."

"I can see this is going to be one of our 'discussions,'" Ann said. "Oh, how I miss the life of the mind."

"So do I." I winced, although I tried not to spend much time thinking about my losses. "In traditional sign theory all signs are meaningful and meant to be read by Christ. Satan forms oppositional patterns by lifting himself up in pride and breaking the communion of Heaven. Satan's original act is repeated by evildoers throughout the time line."

Ann poked me and nodded toward the dogs.

I realized that Baltho and Choc were sitting side by side in front of us, preening, stretching their heads up high—higher—as we looked down at them, as if to make sure that we thought them both the most handsome and important specimens on the planet. "Now, don't follow Satan, you two," I joked. "God is supposed to lift us up, just as he did Jesus on the cross."

Ann crossed her eyes, aware of the irony of my comment.

"Crucifixion precedes resurrection," I replied.

Laughing, Ann called Baltho over to feel his chest. Choc didn't mind a bit. He stood watching and panting. "You'd never know you had a zipped up chest and drain tubes not long ago," she remarked.

Choc came to me for petting.

"Baltho seems to be doing much better in all ways," Ann said.

"I sure hope so," I replied, giving Choc a good rubdown from his head to tail. "I'd hate to have you neglected. It's so good to have dogs that aren't jealous."

"I seem to recall something a professor told us about Old English," Ann added. "He said that when people said, 'I cannot stomach that,' their language was rooted in reality. They literally couldn't stomach something. It made them sick to their stomachs. Which is much stronger than saying, 'I don't like it.'"

"I can't think of any image that is conjured up out of thin air," I said. "Otherwise, our statements have no rooting in the reality of our experience. If we stay rooted, our responses will reflect properly the gut reaction to something that isn't good for us."

"That's the rub," Ann began. "We get messed up because we're socialized to ignore truths we know deep down. Then, when we say we don't like something, it might be nothing more than what we've learned to say, what society dictates, not because it's truly bad for us, or we really don't like it," Ann said.

At that moment, Baltho started coughing, as if he had something caught in his throat, something he couldn't stomach.

Choc started coughing as well, as if to mimic him.

I wondered when they were going to throw up.

But neither of the dogs coughed up a thing. They just coughed, acting as if they were choking.

Ann and I looked at each other and laughed. We wondered if they weren't reacting to our learned discussion with signs of their own.

For a moment Ann stopped laughing and asked, "What pictures do you think they saw that disturbed them?"

"Both of us sitting here yakking and not paying enough attention to them," I replied.

"We couldn't be said to be ignoring them. I'd guess they're bored with our heady discussion. They're telling us they're no longer able to stomach it."

"I'd guess they're sick of it," I said. "After all, no animal can stand too much sitting around."

Ann called Choc to her and started petting him vigorously with both hands. "You aren't plants in the garden, are you?" she remarked.

I did the same with Baltho. By turning slightly and trying to put his forelegs out toward me, he indicated that he wanted to wrestle. But I—more than ever—was scared to go that far. In a soothing but authoritative voice, I said, "Stay calm. I don't want to invite any forebodings—in either of us."

Choc walked over to the front door and barked. He was ready to go home.

"Owned by our dogs," Ann grumbled good-naturedly. She got up to leave.

"You read that sign well," I laughed, bidding them good night. "Someday my prince will come," she said, a phrase she repeated fairly often. I wondered when she'd realize she already had him—in Choc.

Baltho got up. Together we walked to the door. We watched Ann and Choc disappear down the well-lit street toward their home.

Baltho didn't seem to want to go out, as if something were restraining him. I talked with him, asking if he didn't want me to get the leash and take him for a walk. Still, he resisted.

That struck me as odd. If he really were doing well, he would have wanted to bound out with Choc and Ann. Failing that, he would have wanted to go for a walk with me.

"Don't you want to walk past Figgy's and see if he's outside?" I asked. "Maybe he'll come to the sidewalk for a visit."

But Baltho showed no interest in any of my suggestions. He turned and went to lie down on the carpet in front on the couch.

Even though I tried to get him to go out before I shut off the lights and went to bed, he continued to refuse.

Morning

It was a beautiful, sunny morning in June. At seven, Baltho walked eagerly to the back door and wanted to go greet the day. We had just marked our fourth year together. Catching Baltho's joy, I opened the back door and bounded out after him, suddenly realizing that the entire porch and steps were covered with potted plants taken from around the edges of the gardens. Some pots were mine. Some belonged to neighbors.

I managed to avoid falling over the pots but somehow found myself standing upright on the cobbled path at the bottom of the steps. My head was tumbling, my heart rate fast, and my breathing shallow.

Baltho was out in the yard, looking things over. I was glad he hadn't fallen. That would certainly not help his healing process. From what I could recall, Baltho had leaped over the pots, just as he would have done when he was in top shape.

Our HOA vice-president and manager, Adolph had mowed down all the gardens with the lawnmower, rather than do any weeding or hire someone to tend to the yard. Except for the bushes, the gardens were mowed the same height as the grass.

The realization that I could have fallen out my back door and tumbled down the steps had shaken me. Outrage was setting in. I felt the heat in my face and chest. I had kept my word about doing no more gardening work than necessary after the big brouhaha over the HOA's failing to follow the Declarations and Covenants and Rita's demeaning comments about my gardening and budget. Things had been rapidly deteriorating ever since. Weeds sprouted everywhere. People other than me complained about the yard. I figured I'd just let things happen and see if any lights would go on.

Adolph could easily have pushed the pots from the garden edges onto the cobblestone walks so that he could mow everything down, but instead he chose to cover my back porch and steps with them. He knew that Baltho and I bounded out the back door every morning. Was he hoping we'd fall? I'd heard he wasn't keeping up our liability and building insurance. I didn't know this to be a fact, but nothing would surprise me. What did he think would have happened if I'd been seriously hurt by his malicious deeds and sued?

When a woman had slipped on branches and leaves that hadn't been picked up in front of the building in March, I informed the new president, Mark. "I helped the woman get to her feet and told her the name of the president of the HOA. I also showed her where you live."

Mark listened in silence.

"If someone sues over the obvious negligence that has come to characterize this place, they'll win a big settlement," I said. "Our insurance won't cover it."

Mark shrugged. "If we get into trouble, we'll make the HOA funds disappear. Then nobody can get anything from us."

"You think that'll work?" I asked, remembering that he was a mutual fund salesman for a large brokerage in town. "You don't think the plaintiff's lawyers would search out our funds and also go after each of us individually?"

Mark didn't answer. Adolph had come to stand at his side.

"What do you think would happen when we tried to get insurance coverage after such an incident?" I asked.

Neither Mark nor Adolph seemed concerned. They shrugged and laughed. "You're just making more trouble," Adolph said. "Rivas always fix things," he assured me.

I told Baltho, "Stay put. Don't eat anything. I'm going inside for my camera." When I came back outside with it, I tried to steady my hands to snap some pictures. I had a hard time of it because I was so shaken. Finally, I managed to take four or five shots of the pots spread over my porch and steps. I also snapped several pictures of the mowed off gardens.

"I'll bet the bastard charges the HOA for this 'gardening,' above what he charges for regular mowing," I mumbled to myself. "Mona will reimburse him. After all, he hates the job."

I called Baltho back inside. "But we'll never know," I recalled. "We don't get regular spending reports as dictated by law. Nor are the books audited by an outsider. Mona is doing that, and she won't cross the Rivas. They're too powerful. We know how that works."

That afternoon, my friend Helen stopped by. Baltho and I greeted her at the door. I told her what had happened that morning. "I placed a call to Mark and to the Rivas about the incident. They didn't pick up, so I left messages. I also left a message on Adolph's machine," I said. "All the work I've done for years has gone to naught. The perennials that I've planted, many of which I paid for myself, are dying, or being wiped out," I fumed. "This is the final straw."

"We are as flies to wanton boys," Helen intoned. "They kill us for their sport."

"What happened to your positive thinking?" I asked.

Helen didn't respond.

"Since someone—Lear blames the gods—is trying to kills us like flies," I said, "I say we must grab the damned fly swatters out of their hands and swat back."

Helen cracked a smile. She took a seat in one of the winged-back rocking chairs near the front window of my living room. Baltho sat at her side. "You need to calm down. You're only hurting yourself," she said.

I offered her a cup of freshly brewed Darjeeling tea.

"No milk," she said, putting her hand over her cup after I poured her tea. "You know how tea and coffee become toxic when milk is added."

"That isn't good science," I said. "The English have been using milk in their coffee and tea for centuries." I added milk to my cup. "I like Darjeeling with milk. Otherwise, I drink my tea and coffee as is."

All of a sudden, the doorbell rang and rang again. Someone started pounding on my security door and yelling.

I went to see what the ruckus was about. Red-faced and reeking of alcohol, Adolph screamed through the locked door at me. "You don't do anything but raise my blood pressure and cause trouble!" he yelled. "For your information, I never do a thing around here without Riva's approval. Lots of people here hate you, especially Ron and Rita. Don't think otherwise," he said. "They've got connections."

"That sounds like a threat," I said. "Of course, they've got connections."

"You son of a bitch! Let me in! I'll show you some connections at the end of my arm."

"I'll bet you'd try," I said, refusing to unlock the door.

"Do you think you can cause all the trouble you cause and get away with it?" Adolph demanded. "Nobody here cares about the beauty of the grounds. We regard the place as a bedroom community. That's it." He kept on, rambling more and more in his ever-increasing, drunken-booming, manner. Soon, he made no sense at all.

I closed the door, turned, and went back inside.

"You've got to move from here," Helen said. "I don't trust Adolph or the others. These people are sheep. They bleat until you disturb their happy grazing. Then they become violent." She paused. "I could smell the liquor on Adolph's breath even from where I'm sitting, twenty feet from the door. You don't know what other drugs Adolph does."

"I can guess," I said, recalling my neighbor James' assertions of Adolph's love of substances. "I will move," I said, my composure regained, even though my heart felt like it was going to jump out of my chest. "Jessie sold her unit and left," I said. "She told me she didn't feel safe here. She refused to allow her children to be put in danger and was afraid her husband would actually shoot someone."

I recalled how on moving day Mark and Adolph showed up at Jessie's back door and demanded twelve-hundred dollars. The day was sunny and warm. I was sitting outside reading with Baltho lying at my feet.

"For what?" she asked them. "I'm paid up. You signed off on all the papers."

"We made a mistake. You still owe twelve-hundred dollars," Mark said. Adolph nodded in agreement.

They refused to leave until she paid them. Jessie's moving men were there. Mark and Adolph were making a scene.

Jessie grabbed her checkbook, wrote a check for twelve- hundred dollars, and tossed it at Mark. "Now shove off!" she said, pushing them out the door.

It seemed that it was my turn to run. I didn't know how long it would take before I could move. "I can't find another place as easily as someone with ready cash might,"

I reminded Helen. "My finances have been devastated by all my troubles with the Golds. I'll have to allow things to fall into place without trying to force them. That isn't a new lesson for me," I said. "That's what I've always had to do." I paused. "I have to trust the mystery that knits my life together. I'm always taken care of—just not necessarily in ways that I want, or in the time of my choosing."

I didn't know if my answer satisfied Helen. It certainly wasn't the typically American way of doing things. But it was the way of the mystic.

Setback

Soon after I put my feet on the floor that morning, the front doorbell rang. I walked to the door and opened it. Adolph was standing on my stoop. A few weeks had passed since our altercation. He seemed in a good mood. I wondered if his synapses were so burned that he'd forgotten all about the scene. I certainly hadn't. Nor had Helen.

With more than a little glee, he said, "Too bad about our prez, Mark. He thinks he wants to be with men." Adolph seemed to think he was telling me a joke.

I wanted to say something about Adolph's usual depth of understanding, but I knew my efforts would only be wasted.

"I don't know why anyone chooses to have sex with men," he said.

I thought of remarking, "Yes, I've often wondered that about your wife," but instead, I said, "I need to go to the grocery store." I turned to get Baltho. He'd appeared to want to go with me, so I hooked his leash onto his collar, shut the door behind us, and pushed past Adolph still standing on the steps.

The day was overcast, and it was rather cool for August. I wondered if we would have an early frost. The nights seemed to be reflecting the crispness of the coming autumn, more than they usually did at that time of year.

Outside, Baltho and I went through our routine. I helped him get his front legs up onto the back seat of the car. Once his front half was in, he was usually able to lift his back half on his own. Even though he'd had his tumor removed, he still hadn't regained full strength in his legs.

At the grocery store, I ran into my church friend Karen again.

"Must be fate," I said, greeting her.

"Have you heard about Emma Gold?" she asked.

"No," I said. "Through a colleague I heard that her husband entered into a plea bargain with the Colorado Attorney General, but I've tried to stay away from that whole mess."

"Understandable." She paused. "Emma's been diagnosed with cancer."

"So the prophecy's fulfillment begins," I said, mostly to myself.

"John's beside himself. Emma's the light of his life," Karen said.

"And his helpmate in darkness," I muttered. "Sorry, but I can't help it. They've put too many people through hell."

"I do wish you'd come back to church," Karen said. "But I understand that you must follow your own path."

I nodded. I still appreciated the low-key approach of Episcopalians in matters of conscience. "I'm not sure I'll ever go back. I have no problems with mere Christianity, but I have lots of misgivings about organized religion."

"Well you take care of yourself and your dog," Karen said, bidding me goodbye.

When we got back to my townhome, I parked in front of my unit. Baltho didn't seem able to jump down from the car. Although he tried, his front legs shook. I lifted him down and placed him carefully on the street. He seemed heavier than ever. In the bright sun, I noticed that his hair had lost its sheen. More white marked his nose and beard.

In our townhome mailboxes sat letters from the HOA president. Mark announced his resignation, saying he and his wife were selling their unit and going their separate ways. "Oh great," I said. "Adolph will now be the HOA president, vice-president, manager, and God-knows-what-else, HOA Declarations and Covenants be damned." My guess was that another election wouldn't be in the offing. "Now we've gone from poor management to a coup d'état."

I sighed and looked down at Baltho. "You had trouble getting out of the car." I shut the front door and looked around my house. "How much worse can things around here get, Mr. Dog, my dog?" I asked.

Baltho seemed to want to walk. I knew that would help me work out some of my anxiety, but I wondered if he really was up to it. He kept acting like he was, his eyes bright and his manner eager, so I got the leash. I hooked it onto his collar.

At a moderate pace, we headed south and then east. Baltho neither meandered nor galloped along but walked steadily. Little by little our walking distances had lengthened.

He seemed eager to prove himself. Every time I offered to turn the corner and go home, Baltho indicated that he wanted to continue moving forward.

We made it through our neighborhood to 16th Avenue. There we crossed east over I-25 to the South Platte River walk on the other side of the freeway. We stopped at Confluence Park, where the South Platte meets Cherry Creek. This was where Denver began, the center of the gold panning camps. The sun had come out.

Baltho wanted to wade in the river. He was breathing heavily. So was I. Because the water was foamy and smelled of detergents and other chemicals, I was afraid to let him get in.

But Baltho kept edging closer, trying to walk into the river.

Reluctantly, I let him edge his way into the water, thinking he must have felt hot and it would cool him down. As he waded, I thought I detected a faint smile tracing across his face. His eyes looked brighter. His exuberant self was still there. I was relieved. He was becoming good as new.

After fifteen minutes, I suggested we head back home. "I have to make some calls before business hours are over. And we have a couple of counseling appointments in the early evening, right after people get off work. You'll enjoy that," I said. "These are new clients, so we have to be prepared." I was so glad to have them. Things were looking up. I typically got calls but few clients. Some set appointments but never showed up.

Baltho seemed reluctant to get out of the water. Once I convinced him to step out, he kept slipping on the rocks, something he'd never done before. He couldn't find sure footing.

Finally, I waded out into the channel to help hoist him up onto the shore. The rocks were indeed slippery, but not from moss. I almost fell in, thinking to myself that detergents had made the surfaces so slick. Allowing him to wade was probably not at all good, although many people and pets played in the water.

We walked north about a block—when Baltho suddenly froze, as if unable to go further. I tried to coax him forward, gently, but to no avail.

I waited. I tried again. It looked as if he were trying to gather the energy to move, but the muscles in his legs barely twitched. He just stood and looked in the direction that he wanted to go.

That put the fear of God in me. I had never seen anything like it. I looked around. I saw that we were standing outside a machine shop. The front door was open. I let go of Baltho's leash and walked over to call out to someone inside. "Hello! Is anyone here?" I asked. The place seemed cavernous, dark, the temperature sweltering.

A few moments later, a tall, blond man in his late thirties stepped forward into the light of the open door. Immediately, I became aware of some sort of blockage in his heart chakra, but I was too distracted by my dog's problems to pay more attention. "My dog, Baltho, seems unable to walk home," I said, pointing to him still standing like a statue on the sidewalk. "Could I leave him with you, while I walk home to get the car, and return for him? If I hurry, it should take about twenty minutes," I said. "I just live over there, maybe twenty blocks away."

The guy nodded. "I know what it's like. My old pal died a few months ago."

I knew the cause of the heart chakra blockage. Baltho must have sensed that this was a safe place to stop and wait for my return.

"I'll take good care of him," the man assured me. He walked out to help me coax and then, lift, Baltho into the shade of the building. "By the way, I'm Tim," he said. He walked inside and returned with a large green, ceramic bowl of water and a big cedar-filled dog bed, which he placed on the pavement near Baltho. He bent down to see if Baltho would drink. He hugged him.

Baltho didn't want any water. He looked grateful. He managed to drop himself down onto the cedar bed, which I surmised had belonged to the man's dog.

I bent down to hug Baltho and assure him that I would be back just as soon as I could. Internally I was kicking myself for being such a fool to let us go so far from home. Even if Baltho had wanted to keep going, I should have known better.

As my legs carried me home, I kept berating myself. I quickened my pace, glancing often at my watch to count the minutes. When I got to my car, I stuck the key in the door and hopped in. I managed to return to the machine shop seventeen minutes after I'd left.

Baltho was still lying down. He barely picked up his head, but his eyes followed me. I got out of the car, opened the back car door on the street side, and rushed toward him. "Baltho, I'm back."

He didn't stand. That wasn't a good sign. It sent chills down my spine. In the old days he would have jumped up and been eager to go. Even recently he would have risen and walked toward me.

Tim had been standing in the doorway, evidently keeping his eye on Baltho. He came outside and helped me lift him into the back seat of my car.

"I guess the long walks are gone," I said, thinking aloud that I should have been more cautious, despite both Baltho's and my wanting to walk on. "Far too far," I lamented, noting the anger in my voice.

"We get hopeful," Tim said, nodding, as if he knew the scenario too well. "Just take it easy. And don't let either of you get too excited about what you might do. That's a mistake. I made it myself."

Tim handed me his business card. "Call if you need any help, even someone to talk to."

I introduced myself, thanked him, and wished him well. "It would be insensitive to say I hope you'll find a replacement for your dog," I said. "But I hope you'll find another one as good and faithful as he."

I had to turn quickly because I found myself tearing up. Tim was also starting to choke up.

With Baltho panting heavily in the back seat, I drove north and then west toward home.

I kept wondering if Ann would be around so I could get her to assist in carrying Baltho inside. If she wasn't, I'd have to look for someone else. I didn't know if anyone strong enough might be there in the middle of the day. My elderly neighbors wouldn't much help.

By the time we pulled into my spot in front of my townhome, Baltho seemed to have gathered some strength. He insisted on getting down from the seat and walking rather carefully and slowly into the house on his own.

In my chest, I felt the terrible weight of guilt. I should never have gotten so carried away. After all, I was supposed to be the one with greater intelligence, greater ability to see the bigger picture. "I should have been more cautious. Much more cautious," I lamented.

When Baltho got inside, he dropped down in front of the couch, as if he couldn't go any further. His breathing was fast and shallow. I went to the kitchen for his water and placed it before him. Again, he refused to drink.

"Would you like some yogurt?" I asked, fetching a bowl of cold yogurt and placing it before him. He refused it. "How about some cold chicken?" He turned that down too. "I could warm it. Would that make a difference?" I petted him, fearing aloud what damage I'd done. "You were doing so well," I whispered.

I phoned my clients and rescheduled, saying that I was sorry but I'd had an emergency and couldn't see them that evening.

Then I called the vet. He reiterated his diagnosis that Baltho was getting old. "He's become over-stressed. If he doesn't improve with rest, bring him in." Within a few hours, Baltho seemed better. He walked slowly to the kitchen and whimpered to go out into the courtyard. As he slowly made his way down the back steps, he seemed almost normal.

He snooped around the yard, especially the shrubs and bushes that might harbor some nice animal odors. He looked up into the trees and onto the tops of the fence to see if he could spot some squirrels. He used to love to race after them. He lifted his leg on the crab apple tree and then decided to lie down in the deep shade of the huge cottonwood at the back of the garden. The cool ground and mowed perennials must have felt good.

Since the rules forbidding animals to be out on their own for more than a few minutes weren't being enforced, I figured Baltho could rest there. Such rules could be relaxed, since he wasn't well and could do no damage that Adolph hadn't already done. Unlike some of the dogs in the complex, Baltho had never dug or torn anything up in all the years he'd been with me. He'd stepped on only a few flowers. Since I'd done most of the gardening—when it was done—and had shopped carefully for quality plants at the best price—I figured he had the right. Because he had no appetite, I didn't have to worry that he might find some poisoned morsel to devour.

Still, I worried. I tried to coax Baltho inside, but he got only as far as the crab apple fifteen-feet from my back door. He dropped down and wanted to remain. It was cool there. I would fight for his right to remain where he was comfortable.

I went inside, leaving the security door open so he could come in when he was ready. Between some phone calls, I kept walking to the door to check on him. He hadn't moved an inch.

I could see his chest rising and falling, but not so fast as it had, a good sign.

When I walked outside to try to get Baltho in the house again, I noticed several flies gathering around him and landing. Usually he would move enough to scare them away.

As I continued to observe, I noticed more flies. I decided to make Baltho come inside. I placed my arms beneath his chest and lifted him so he could walk. "You don't need flies biting you."

Rita opened her back door. "Tom, would you get your dog inside?" she said, her tone nasty.

"What do you think I'm doing?" I asked angrily, recalling how often Adolph's dog was out, digging up the gardens and chewing up everything that he could get his mouth on. I also recalled how, when he was president and manager, Ron had let one of the renter's dogs tear up the flower beds near my back door. Only after I complained several times, because the dog had dug a huge hole that it could lie in, did Ron finally tell them to cut it out.

Slowly, Baltho followed me inside to the living room floor, where he dropped down with a thud, his breathing fast and shallow again. The old grace had vanished, to be replaced by conflict between his desires and what was possible, given the body that he wore.

I turned on the television. I surfed channels. I heard something about an accident that seemed to involve Princess Diana in Paris. No one knew what actually had taken place. As the afternoon went on, a newscaster announced that Diana was dead. She had been seriously injured in a freak auto accident in a Paris tunnel. Her lover,

Dodi Al Fayed, had been with her. Apparently he and their driver had been killed.

Details about the accident remained sketchy, although rumors began to multiply. Had these people been murdered because the Royals wanted to get rid of Diana, who was fraternizing with the wrong sort? Did the Al Fayed family's other enemies want Dodi and Diana out of the way? Was Diana pregnant with Dodi's baby?

I could hardly take in what I was hearing. Although everyone was trying, no one seemed to be doing a good job of reading these signs.

I became glued to the television. It was a good thing that I'd cancelled my clients. Not only had I experienced an emergency, but so had much of the world.

Everything about the accident seemed surreal, bigger than life, yet somehow not real—as if the newscasters and others were trying to put over some terrible hoax.

By evening, however, the reality of this tragedy seemed to have sunk in. We were past the denial. Friends had phoned to ask if I had heard the news, and, if I had, what I thought. Did I believe it was just an accident, or was something more sinister at work?

I wondered the same about my dog, Baltho. He was lying a few yards from me on the living room carpet. His breathing remained fast and shallow.

Winter

Summer rolled into fall, leaves turning golds, reds, oranges, then spiraling down, crisp and brown. In corners where they weren't brushed up, they molded. Now and then, little snows swept through, melting soon after they fell. From infancy through my mid-twenties, I'd found our winters snowier and colder than they were now.

Baltho continued to hang on to life, but, while I couldn't say he was doing well, he didn't seem worse. I wondered what I would do when the inevitable happened.

One morning in early December, with this question like a shadow whispering in my ear, I walked to the door to see if the *Denver Post* had arrived. I couldn't let the darkness take over.

As I unfolded the paper, my eyes fell on a full color picture of John Gold, accompanied by an article in which he recommended that everyone make an altar for home use and meditate daily before it, just as he did. "You can put on it everything that is important to you—pictures of loved ones, meaningful objects, stones, plants," he said. He was teaching classes on this.

"Lots you know about genuine spirituality," rushed from my mouth.

Brian called to see how I was doing. "Laura and I have been wondering how you were," he said.

"I'm OK," I said, "but can't say I'm doing well. Baltho is still having problems."

"You know you're welcome to come visit us any time you want."

I asked about the kids. "They're growing," Brian said. "Laura is over-working, as usual. We hardly see her. I'm trying to further my publishing enterprises." He paused. "Really, Tom, why don't you pack Baltho in the car and come up?" he urged.

"I'll think about it," I said, thanking him for his offer.

"By the way, have you heard that Penelope had to give Victor back to his dad?" Laura asked, picking up another receiver.

"What happened?" I asked.

"He kept becoming more violent and threatening her," Laura said.

I was going to say something about stoning the prophets, but decided to keep my mouth shut and concentrate on my ongoing search for various healing modalities for my dog. Even though he and I didn't try any more long walks together, I still believed that he might be made right—or at least put on a firmer path in that direction.

One clear day, I happened to be in my psychic friend Marilyn's neighborhood near City Park. I stopped at her house and rang the bell. I had lifted Baltho into the car so that he could have a bit of an outing. "All I can tell you is he doesn't feel very well," Marilyn said. She didn't have time to chat. "I've got to go pick up Bill," her boyfriend. She walked me out to the car to see Baltho.

"Are you sure you don't feel he's been poisoned?" I asked. "I've watched him like a hawk ever since my neighbor alerted me to her suspicions regarding that Mexican poison."

"I don't feel it," Marilyn said, running her hand down Baltho's back.

"Do you pick up *anything*?" I asked.

"The vet tells you he's getting old. He doesn't feel well. Try what you can—that's all I can say."

I tried Jin Shin Jyutsu, healing touch, along with more energy balancing—from various healers. Most modalities seemed to help for a few days, granting Baltho a little more energy. But nothing gave him back his old, bounding, clownish self. I had so hoped that removing the lipoma from his chest and giving him Rimadyl, along with glucosamine-chondroitin, and dog vitamins would set him right.

Quietly, I would lock the door and sneak off for long walks on my own. It was as if Baltho knew that I needed to walk far longer and faster than he could manage. Short walks across the street and back, or around part of the block, he could handle. Now and then, we'd see Figgy, who would look at us on the sidewalk in front of his new home. Rarely did he venture out to see us. "I guess you don't want to take any chances," I'd tell him, part scolding, part disappointed.

By Christmas, Baltho rarely followed me to the door when I walked to it. He would look up at me with eyes that no longer seemed to register a great deal, as if he was too tired even to try. More and more, I had to coax him to go on walks longer than a hundred feet.

Faithfully I fed him his vitamins, his glucosamine-chondroitin capsules, and Rimadyl. I laid hands on him, hoping I could give him vital energy as I had Oriana, my first Afghan years before. She recovered from being bounced off five cars on Federal Boulevard, even though the vet told me to take her home to die. Miracles did happen. I hoped against hope to witness another.

When we had a deep freeze with four inches of snow that covered the ground for days, I realized that Adolph had once again failed to winterize our irrigation system. Every year I had to tell him to be sure to get that done, harp at him several times, and then go higher up the chain of command before he finally moved to get someone out to do the job. An irrigation systems man usually arrived in the midst of our cold snaps.

If a pipe burst, it would probably be just outside my unit, or less likely, Mona's because the water came from our two places. Now and then I had a premonition of a pipe bursting outside my unit. With incompetence and corruption in charge, I wished to God I hadn't bought my particular unit but one far away from the irrigation water supply.

I called the Rivas about the problem. "We've had ten days of subzero weather. The water in the irrigation pipes is getting colder as we speak. It's probably about to freeze and flood someone's unit, probably mine," I said. Rita listened. "Adolph says he never does anything without your permission. I shouldn't have to act as his babysitter," I said, ending the conversation.

An irrigation systems specialist came out that afternoon, needing access to my unit and Mona's to winterize the system.

My anxiety over various issues kept ratcheting up. Because of the snow and ice, I wasn't walking much to help relieve it. By eight that night, I felt so exhausted that I went to bed early and fell into a deep sleep.

"Tommy, what have you done to me?" John Gold cried, his voice bursting with desperation.

"What?" I asked. I thought I was holding the phone, but I had to fumble to find it. It was on the nightstand. For a few moments, I didn't know what was going on. I looked at the clock. It was three in the morning

The phone hadn't rung. Strange. I would have sworn I'd answered it. Gold was on the other end.

By now, I was wide awake. Baltho lay sleeping fitfully on the floor beside me. He snored. His feet twitched as if he were trying to run—dash away from all his troubles. If the phone had rung, Baltho would have noticed. He would have been awake himself.

The phone rang. I was sure it was ringing this time.

I reached over to the nightstand and grabbed it. "Hello," I said. I tried not to sound groggy.

"Tommy, what have you done to me?" This time it was John Gold on the other end. I was sure of it. His voice sounded desperate, as if he'd been weeping.

"I haven't done anything to you. You've done it to yourself," I said. "You should have remembered that sooner or later all of us reap what we've sown."

Gold hung up.

Spring Thaw

As the crocuses, daffodils, and tulips began to emerge through the wood chips, Baltho seemed to perk up, as if he too might blossom. I wasn't about to attempt long walks with him— ever—but he seemed eager to walk down and around the block again.

He wanted to lie out in the grass of the courtyard in the warm spring sun. His eyes followed the robins hopping around in search of worms. He seemed to enjoy the song of the sparrows. The squirrels even caught his eye. Now and then, he would get up and walk over to view them chattering along the fence, eating garbage that they had found in the bins, strewing it everywhere. He didn't attempt to chase them. Nor did he touch the food they dropped. I watched carefully. In his good days, he certainly would have.

When Mona let out her coal-colored toy poodle, Sparkles, she worried if she saw Baltho there, even though I was almost always present myself—or just about to return. Sparkles had appeared in the alley some years before as a puppy, so Mona adopted her. Now that Sparkles had gone blind, and appeared increasingly helpless, Mona feared Baltho might attack her. "Just don't let him hurt her," she'd plead. I thought maybe she was so caught up in her own dog's failing health that she couldn't see that Baltho was no better off than Sparkles.

As a rule, Baltho still managed to get up and sniff at Sparkles, then leave her alone and lie down again. He'd done that even when he was feeling better. Despite Mona's worries, he had never shown any aggressiveness toward Sparkles at all. I never expected him to. That wasn't my dog—not Baltho.

One day, I was inside using the bathroom. I had left Baltho outside for a few minutes. I heard my neighbor James yelling at the top of his lungs. To hear him yelling about something wasn't unusual. But this time, I heard him yelling at Baltho, scolding him.

Without washing my hands, I hurried out to see what was going on. James liked Baltho, but today he was very angry. I gathered from James' fit that he had opened his back door so he could let some fresh air inside. Baltho had noticed and got up to pay him a visit. Finding some shred of his old self, he smelled a package of hot dogs on James' kitchen counter. He managed to scarf a couple of them before James noticed what had happened.

"A couple of hot dogs probably wouldn't hurt him," I said. "He doesn't have much of an appetite anymore."

James responded, "They weren't fresh."

I asked, "How old were they?"

James said, "They were starting to smell. I was going to throw them out. That's why they were on the counter." Pacing the cobblestones, and muttering, James then confessed. "They were slimy and green. I've said it. I hope to God they didn't hurt Baltho, since he's sick and about to die." I could tell he was drunk, and probably high on something.

I glanced at my watch. It was four, so the vet would be getting ready to leave for the day. "Keep an eye on Baltho. I'm going inside to call Dr. Smith. I'll see what he says." It felt like I talked with the vet more than I talked with my sister Vickie, whom I spoke with at least once a week. I knew I saw the vet more often than I saw her or any of my friends.

Dr. Smith told me that Baltho, even though not doing well nowadays, "probably won't be hurt by a couple of old hot dogs." He said Baltho's heart rate was a bit slow, and he wasn't very energetic, but he didn't seem alarmed. "Keep an eye on him. If you need to call after hours, call our emergency service number," he said. "Someone is available at nights and over the weekends."

I hung up. I walked back outside. Baltho was vomiting. I figured this was his way of purging tainted meat from his system.

But he kept vomiting. James, who was pacing, but watching, began to scream and cry. He confessed that Baltho "ate an entire package—a family pack of rotten hot dogs," James cried. "I know it's gonna kill him! I've killed your dog!" he screamed. "The same thing happened to our family dog. When I was thirteen, friends and I fed him a big package of rotten hot dogs, and he died."

I watched Baltho vomit more. All that was coming up now was greenish yellow bile.

I hoped that was the end of it.

But it wasn't. He kept vomiting bile.

"Help me get him into the car," I told James.

We managed to get Baltho into the vehicle. I sped to the vet. It was nearly five, but he would still be there if I hurried.

Dr. Smith examined him. He said Baltho had pancreatitis and gave me some pills to administer "every four hours, even through the night," he said. "If those don't stop the vomiting by morning, bring him in."

During the night, Baltho's vomiting slowed down, and then ceased. He began sipping a little water, although he didn't want to eat anything.

After a few days, he began to eat a little again. He'd not had a great appetite for the last year, but at least he was eating something.

Again, he wanted to spend most of his time lying in the grass. So I would take him out with me and stay for as long as he wanted, watching him—scrying like a hawk ready to descend on anyone, anything, that threatened him. I swore if Rita dared say a word, I'd walk over and knock her for a loop.

For days and days, James moaned. "You're going to blame me for killing your dog. I just know Baltho's going to die. I've killed him!" He seemed drunk and high all the time now, blubbering, stumbling, and crying about murdering my dog.

Pancreatitis can be deadly. I hoped we'd caught it in time, and there would be no repercussions. Dr. Smith had given me hope. But I worried.

I said to James, "Be sure to keep your back door shut at all times and do not, I repeat, do not let Baltho in." I paused to let my words sink in. "If you make the slightest mistake, you'll be sorry. I will go after you. I'm not a violent man, but I swear to God, I will do what I have to do."

Dream

I walked into my living room and found Baltho's neck and head lying on the carpet. I stooped down to take what remained of him in my arms. I held the neck and head up to my chest. "Baltho! What happened? Where's the rest of you? Where's your body?"

The dream went fuzzy, as if the projector was shorting out.

Then, things resumed. I saw myself clearly, going about my business. I stood, interacting with people in my living room. Baltho emerged from the back of the house and walked boldly into the dining room. Happy and well again, he pranced over to me. I was standing—talking with people.

Shocked, I gasped, and bent to hug him to me. His neck and head were reattached to a good body. He looked as he had when I'd first adopted him—energetic, healthy, his hair silky, and his eyes radiant.

Through my tears I cried, "I thought you were dead!"

I woke, shaken—but hopeful.

Baltho would somehow resurrect as good as new. That's what the dream meant. All the things I was doing for him—the treatments, the medications, the prayers, the love—would finally pay off. I wondered if the miracle would happen only after it appeared that all hope was gone—that he was, from all appearances, dead.

When I administered his meds I told him of the dream. "You'll be well soon, Mr. Dog. I've glimpsed the future.

You can believe me," I'd say, hoping to reassure him—and bolster my courage and faith.

I had to get back to my writing. Creativity was an essential element of my calling. Writing would help me focus and alleviate my anxiety. Perhaps poetry was best. I could center for several hours and move to something else. Longer pieces required more lengthy periods of attention that I just couldn't maintain.

I kept reminding myself of the promise delivered by the dream. All the time and money that I was spending on Baltho's health would bring results. I had dreamed it. I knew prophetic dreams when I had them. They had a reality about them that was unlike other dreams and nightmares.

"You'll see, Doggus," I often repeated, using the name that my sister Vickie and her kids sometimes called him. "You'll be as good as new."

Recovery

I kept looking for signs of renewed life in Baltho. He still wanted to spend time outside, there among the flowers, squirrels, and birds.

I never saw Sparkles outside now. "Is Sparkles all right?" I asked Mona the next time I saw her.

"Sparkles died," she said. While I didn't admire Mona's going along with the machinations of Ron and Rita, I felt sorry for her. She was vulnerable to their schemes, and like many modern Americans, didn't stick her neck out. I knew how much Mona loved that dog, even as Sparkles slowly but surely fell apart. "There must be some goodness in Mona, somewhere," I told myself. "She loved her dog."

Even as the heat of the early summer came on, Baltho wanted to remain outside as much as possible. It was growing too hot to remain there during the middle of the day, so I made Baltho come in at eleven a.m. He had to remain inside till early evening when the heat had dissipated. Then I would let him out again.

One day, I noticed how the flies were gathering about him, refusing to leave him alone. Poor dog, he didn't even try to flick them off or bite at them.

I walked over and helped him up. I made him come inside with me. I decided that I'd better examine him to see that he didn't have any sores. I didn't see anything out of order.

A few days later I realized that he was biting his paws. He was hardly able to stand on them.

I took a close look and found that the flies had bitten up inside his pads and laid eggs, which were hatching into maggots. The insides of his toes looked raw and red.

Again, we visited the vet. He cleaned Baltho's pads and gave me a tube of antibiotic ointment to spread on them after I peroxided them every few hours. Dr. Smith said this wasn't unusual. "It happens when dogs spend lots of time outside, especially old dogs that lack the energy to run the flies off." He also gave me a ten-day supply of oral antibiotics to administer every eight hours.

"Baltho, you just can't spend much time outside—no matter how much you want to," I concluded. "You don't have the energy to fight off predators—of any kind. I'll go out with you, watch you walk around a few minutes, until you relieve yourself. But after that, you'll have to come back inside with me."

Shortly after he finished the round of antibiotics for his toes, Baltho's pancreatitis returned. I had no idea why. He'd eaten nothing to bring it on. But he began to vomit bile again. I took him to the vet and got more pills for it, which I administered.

Every time we went to the vet now, I had to find a neighbor, usually Ann, to help me lift Baltho into the car and out again. He just couldn't do it on his own. His body was like a dead weight. He could offer me neither help nor resistance.

In July, our usual summer heat wave arrived. The days blazed, the rose blossoms looked like they'd been thrown into a broiler, and our nights no longer cooled down.

Baltho's pads still looked raw—despite weeks of peroxiding and administering the antibiotic ointment. He wasn't healing well. I noticed that he'd acquired a rather bad smell, faintly like rotting meat.

One of my clients complained that he didn't want Baltho in the room with him. "He smells sour," he said.

Poor dog. I had to put him in the kitchen while the client was there.

I kept trying to administer some therapeutic touch, sending healing into Baltho's body, mind, and spirit.

He'd lie there and glance up at me, as if grateful for the attention.

When other clients came, Baltho would lie in the dining room rather than trying to get near them. He must have known his odor wasn't something people wanted to be around. I didn't notice it much. He was my dog. He'd always be mine—no matter what.

When my sister Vickie and her kids came to visit, we decided to take Baltho out to the courtyard and give him a bath. Kyle, who was maybe eight, laughed and pointed at Baltho's erection, which I'd not observed for months and months, probably years. Maybe that meant he was feeling better, his vital energies returning.

"Baltho's old and sick. Stop making fun of him. You'll be old someday yourself," Vickie scolded. "It's a natural occurrence. You'll see when you get older." She cocked an eye at her son, whose face was showing disapproval.

"Poor old thing," Vickie said, to be repeated by Kyle and Kelsie, as they dried him. Kyle kissed his forehead. Kelsie followed. We helped him hobble back inside.

"We love you, no matter what," Kyle said.

"We won't disown you like Grandma did Tom," Kelsie added.

He smelled so much better. I hoped a good bath in the summer heat would make him feel better too. He'd be both cleaner and cooler.

Baltho seemed happier and a little more energetic, but perhaps the reason was mostly that Vickie and the kids were there. Family cheered him up.

In fact, he wanted to walk that night, taking us all to the front door. I attached his leash. With each of us taking a turn holding it, Kelsie, Kyle, Vickie, and I walked him slowly around the block.

As we turned the corner, I spotted a raccoon crouching under an elm tree ten feet away from us. Taking Baltho's leash from Kyle, I signaled for the others to move on, quietly. I hoped Baltho wouldn't notice him, because he'd want to give chase if he did. That would have been his reaction in the past. After all, he was a sight hound.

Baltho turned his head toward the raccoon. Surely, he saw him. Yet, he didn't react, didn't even tug on the leash.

All of us walked on by—then back home, without further incident.

When I first got Baltho, the kids loved having him jump up on the couch where they could brush and comb his hair. They draped some of the Egyptian silk scarves—of iridescent blues, greens, purples, and apricots—that I'd brought back from a trip to Egypt around his head and neck. They covered their own heads and shoulders with the scarves that were left over.

We snapped pictures of the kids and Baltho clowning together. We couldn't figure out whether Baltho, the kids, or we adults enjoyed it most.

Reminiscing on these times, I said, "I hope Baltho is resurrecting. I dreamed that he would."

"We sure hope you're right, don't we, kids," Vickie replied.

Kelsie and Kyle nodded quietly, seriously, as if more than a little gloom hung like a pall over the room.

The next day we decided to make stuffed bell peppers for dinner.

Memories of how much Baltho had loved stuffed peppers came to mind. In the past, while the peppers were cooling, and I wasn't in the room to guard them, he'd gotten his front paws up onto the stove top so that he could stand there and eat the stuffing out of them.

The first time this had happened, I'd made two cake pans full of peppers which I left uncovered on the stove. I went upstairs to work on the computer.

When I returned, every single pepper had the mound of rice, ground meat, onions, and seasonings eaten down to the rims. I worried about the diced onions in them, which are toxic to dogs. I worried that the stuffing must have burned his mouth because it was hot, straight out of the oven. But nothing bad seemed to come of it. If his mouth had been burned, Baltho certainly never acted like anything was amiss.

On at least two other occasions, he sampled the stuffing when I forgot and left the peppers out to cool.

But now, even stuffed peppers did not seem to hold much interest. We'd made some peppers just for him. They had only a hint of onions in the stuffing. The kids and I broke these up into Baltho's dish. "Mr. Dog, look what we made for you, your favorite," we said.

He nibbled a little but left most.

"Maybe he wanted more onions," Kyle suggested.

Baltho lumbered to the living room and let his body drop down on the carpet. Vickie, Kelsie, Kyle, and I sat at the dining room table, picking at our food, as if our own enjoyment of eating had gone.

Shortly after my family left for home, Helen dropped by to see how I was doing. I made the mistake of telling her that I was spending about six dollars a day on medications for Baltho.

"You're more concerned about that dog than anything else in the world," Helen said. She shook her head. "I think it's terrible that Americans care more about their pets than about the children who are starving, even in this country."

"Droves of us do care—but our animals are like our children. And they're right here in front of us." I paused, hoping that another view might enlighten her. "It would be a great sin not to care about our animals. We can do something about them. We can't always do much about children, especially when they belong to other people. We certainly cannot re-raise them, and erase all the bad that their parents have done—although many of us try."

Helen became silent as stone.

I wasn't sure if she accepted my argument—or if she knew that she'd only earn further defense from me if she went on.

"People's priorities are different, not worse or better," I said, seeing her to the door.

Many times I had thought about how far I would go to make Baltho whole, how much time and money I would spend. I preferred not to have to entertain such thoughts. But I knew in my heart that I would spend a fortune that I didn't have—if I thought for a moment that he might be brought back to health.

Starry Night

A July heat spell set in, stressing plant and animal life alike. I continued to refuse Baltho access to the outdoors when the sun was up and the flies were active. But after the sun went down and the weather cooled, I let him out to lie in the common area. The flies that swarmed around him during the day left him alone at night. I checked to make sure.

Meanwhile, the Heart Talk Café had fallen apart. The old chemistry that Marilyn and I had enjoyed with our acupuncturist and O.M.D. Ron didn't happen with anyone else. As with my earlier attempt to start a loose-knit group of holistic healers, I found that creating a team that works well together is hard. The Heart Talk Café had been very popular for a while, but it never brought me many clients. Nor had my forms of networking.

The few counselees that I had filtered in sporadically. I worried that those who did come might complain about Baltho's smell or the fact that he didn't seem well. A healer must keep the atmosphere of his practice as safe and comfortable as possible—otherwise, people who are already stressed become more agitated.

Fortunately, I wasn't a big spender. I'd never lived lavishly. I had invested in mutual funds whenever I'd had extra money. They were doing well, so I could sell some of them.

I hoped to figure out something that would generate income. I'd never given up on my academic pursuits. My studies and writing were important. I decided to make the Milton book my top priority. It would provide an entrée back into my academic profession. I'd found already that not being a professor at a university made getting the study published much more difficult than it would have been otherwise. On the back burner, I continued to work on a number of poems and more popular books—a novel and some body, mind, and soul studies. Those held money-making potential. Once they were published, they would also bring in counseling clients.

To get my book about Milton ready for publication meant blocking out long hours to read the latest scholarship that I had missed. I had to incorporate those thoughts into the text that I'd been working on for years. Milton scholarship is especially daunting because Milton's knowledge was vast and deep. So is the scholarship. If I'd held a university professorship, I would have had the support to do this—in the form of sabbaticals and release time, as well as a steady salary with benefits.

Since I was keeping long hours, working steadily from morning until night, except for some short breaks—mostly now on my writing—I often let Baltho remain outside till one or two in the morning. That's what he desired. I left the back door open and had my desk near the window. I could keep an eye on the well-lit yard. Baltho never budged once he'd settled, never ate a thing outdoors. When I finally decided to call it quits for the evening, I would go to the door and call him in.

One night late in the month, I turned off the computer and went downstairs. I walked outside. The air was warmer than upstairs, which was cooled by the air conditioner and fans. I looked up. How clear the night sky was, how unusually starry, despite the city lights.

Baltho did not want to come in. I kept coaxing him. He whimpered a little, as if to say, "Please let me stay. I want to be left alone."

"You're not going to spend the night outside," I said. I was kind but firm. I hadn't given him any Rimadyl for a few days because he seemed to be having a little pancreatitis again. Now and then, he vomited a little. I was afraid of overmedicating him.

"I want you with me so I can keep an eye on you," I explained. "Come on Baltho. Come inside." I bent down and stroked his head, pausing tenderly on his long, silky ears. I kept talking to him. "You must come inside. You can return to the gardens in the morning."

Finally, he got up and plodded into the kitchen. Just as soon as he got into the light, I realized he was covered in dust and leaves and dry grass. They were strewn all along the route that he'd taken. During various breaks from the book, I had gone on a cleaning rampage. Over the past few days, I'd swept and mopped the vinyl floors, vacuumed the carpets, and polished the furniture. I'd even cleaned the refrigerator.

"Hold still," I said. I began pulling the debris out of his hair. "Dog, you've made such a mess of my nice clean house, not to mention your own hair."

Baltho began whimpering, trying to pull away so he could hobble into the carpeted rooms and lie down. "Oh dog," I sighed, letting him go. I followed him into the dining room to the back window that looked into an alcove. With a thud, he dropped down on the carpet.

I bent to examine him. He still whimpered a little, as if in pain.

"I'll get your meds," I said, petting him. He tried to reach out and touch me feebly with his front paw. "You'll feel better soon," I assured him. "I shouldn't have let you go without the Rimadyl too, I suppose. I didn't want to overmedicate you."

I went to fetch his pills and return. Placing them in the back of his throat, I closed his mouth over them. He finally swallowed. I held his head, stroked it, and looked into his eyes, bending down to touch my cheek to his. "You'll feel better soon."

He continued to whimper, still touching me with his front paw. I held it in my hand. It wasn't like him to express so much discomfort. He was always a good soldier.

I glanced at my watch. It was two-thirty a.m. I didn't know what to do. I wondered if I should take him to the emergency vet and have him looked at.

I considered getting the air mattress and making a bed in the dining room beside him, as I did when Vickie and her kids visited. That way he wouldn't have to move. He could touch me as much as he wanted, and I would hold his paw.

He seemed to calm down. I was tired and knew that I would rest better in my bed. I decided to turn the lights off and go upstairs.

As soon as the Rimadyl took effect, I told myself, he'd gather up strength and lumber up the stairs to sleep on the floor beside me. If he didn't feel up to it, he could remain where he was. I would take him to the vet in the morning.

I hugged and petted him again. He whimpered more.

Again, I wondered if I should haul him to the emergency vet.

I persuaded myself that he would be better just as soon as the medication kicked in.

Finally, I stood up, turned off the lights, and went upstairs to get ready for bed.

After brushing and flossing, then undressing, I pushed the bedroom door almost closed, so that Baltho could nose it open when he finally came upstairs. I switched the overhead light off and got into bed.

Nightmares continually woke me from a fitful sleep. Around four thirty, I started, totally awake. I'd heard a couple of thumps, each separated by a few moments or so, even over the noise of the air conditioner. Baltho must have knocked a floor lamp over, then something else. I would pick things up in the morning, I fell back into a fitful sleep.

Because I was sleeping even worse than before, I climbed out of bed at five. Baltho still hadn't come upstairs. That worried me. Except for the time he was confined to the kitchen to recover from surgery, he had almost always managed to get upstairs before dawn.

As soon as I hit the lower landing I spotted Baltho lying in front of the couch, only a few feet from the bottom of the stairs. His mouth was open, his tongue falling from it. It looked as though he was staring—but at nothing. I knelt and felt him. He was still warm. I tried to shake him awake, but he didn't move. I pushed on his chest to see if I could get him to breathe. I could not. Baltho was dead.

Trying to contain what felt like hysteria, I looked at my watch. I couldn't read the time. When my eyes finally focused, I realized it was too early to call anyone. I had to try to figure out what to do.

I kept holding Baltho and rocking. "If I'd known you were dying, I'd have let you mess up the whole house," I cried. "I didn't know! I thought you were going to get well! I didn't know! Mr. Dog, I am so sorry!" I wailed.

I blamed myself, wondering what I could have—should have—done. Should I have demanded more invasive lab tests? If I had found that Baltho had cancer, would I have put him through chemotherapy and radiation? Even then, that would only have prolonged his life for a little while.

What had happened? Had he never really gotten over the pancreatitis? Had the lipoma been a malignant tumor, after all? Or was Baltho just old, with his body giving out?

I was lost in a maze. I knew I couldn't change things, no matter how hard I wished. I had watched others go through blaming themselves after someone they loved had passed away.

At five-thirty a.m., I picked up the phone to call Marilyn. Her mind wasn't clear yet. "I didn't sleep well," she mumbled. "I had a fitful night."

"Baltho's dead!" I said, hysteria threatening again.

"Are you sure he's dead?" she asked.

"Yes, I'm sure he's dead," I said, feeling like screaming at her. I needed to scream at someone.

"Maybe you can resuscitate him," she said. She reiterated the fact that she hadn't slept well herself. "I knew something was wrong. But I couldn't figure out who was in trouble. Or what was going on."

"Baltho hasn't been dead for long—he isn't stiff yet. He must have just died." I too rambled, struggling to make sense of things.

"I knew something was wrong last night," Marilyn repeated. "I couldn't figure out what it was. I didn't know who was in trouble. I finally conked out on the couch, leaving Bill to sleep upstairs alone."

"The first thump I heard," I said, "must have been when Baltho tried to make it up the stairs to me. The second must have happened when he staggered over to the couch and fell again."

"I knew there was something wrong," Marilyn said, repeating herself as she continued to try to reconstruct her memories. "Every time I would start to fall asleep, I would wake up a few minutes later. I don't think I slept more than a couple of hours, if that."

After Marilyn and I hung up, I paced and stared into space. I knew only vaguely that I was in my living room sitting on the couch with my dead Baltho lying at my feet. I felt like I was dying. "My dog, my animal companion, my best friend, Mr. Dog, is dead," I repeated over and over again, rocking.

At seven a.m., I began calling my family to blurt out the news. My nephew Kyle answered the phone.

"Baltho's dead," I blurted.

No sound came from the other end. Then I heard wailing that got louder and more out of control.

My sister Vickie took the receiver. "I wish we lived in Denver. You know we can't immediately come to help or comfort you, except by phone," she said. "We'll come as soon as we can. That probably can't be till next weekend."

I hemmed and hawed over calling my mother, whom I hadn't talked with for nearly two years. It was early. I did it anyway.

"Do you want me to come stay with you?" she asked, as if nothing had ever come between us.

"No, no," I mumbled. "Vickie can't come till next weekend. I'll get through it."

"Maybe I can get Diane to take me."

"I'll be all right." I wasn't sure my mother could give me any comfort. I just didn't trust her anymore.

When the vet opened at eight, I called to find out what to do with Baltho's body. The receptionist said they offered a cremation service." You can bring Baltho's body here, and the cremation service will pick it up this morning."

I went to my door and walked outside. The day was overcast and muggy. I knocked on Ann's door. I noticed the echoing sound as if her home was vacant. The world was fracturing, threatening to break apart.

Ann answered. She knew by the look on my face that something was wrong. "Something's happened to Baltho," she said.

I nodded. "I need your help with his body."

Ann followed me to my house. I could not help but notice the acrid smell coming from his body and his still-open eyes. His tongue hung from his opened mouth. His hair looked matted and dull.

She helped me wrap him in a sheet and carry him out to the car. I could hardly stand the dead weight. He felt so much heavier than he'd ever felt, even when he was at his sickest.

"Do you want me to go with you?" she asked. Her face looked terrible. She was reflecting my pain.

"No, I must do this by myself," I said, almost breaking down again.

With Baltho's body secured on the back seat, I drove to the strip mall where the vet was located. The receptionist had told me to pull around to the side. She'd meet me at the steel door that opened to the outside.

One of Emily Dickinson's finest poems began reciting itself in my mind. The poem ends, "First—Chill—then Stupor—then the letting go—"

I managed to stumble out of the car, as if I were drunk. I made my way to the steel door. I'd never noticed it before. My heart was dropping to the pit of my stomach.

The receptionist opened the door. I knew her name, but I drew only a blank each time I tried to retrieve it from memory.

"The cremation service will be here any minute," she said.

Within minutes, a medium-sized, yellow truck pulled up. It was unmarked. I wished he'd taken longer. I wasn't ready to let go.

A man in his thirties jumped down. He walked to the back of the truck and opened the doors. He turned around and looked at me. "Where's the body?" he asked.

Still in a daze, I pointed to my car.

The man walked over and opened the back door on the driver's side. He bent down and gently lifted Baltho out. He carried him to the truck and placed him inside a large, coffin-like, container in the back.

I heard the receptionist ask if I wanted to take the sheet home or leave it to be disposed of. My ears were roaring. I knew her name—but I still couldn't remember it. I was going through the motions dictated by duty. My being felt as lifeless as Baltho's body. This was the last time I'd see it. He wasn't there. I knew that. His body was an empty husk that had once housed him, my dog.

By now, I was blubbering so badly that I had no idea what I was saying. I too was disconnecting from my body, which moved in ever-slowing motion. I could feel my soul fleeing, searching the ether for the soul of my dog.

Suddenly, I found myself with my arms empty, except for the green sheet that I had wrapped Baltho in. "It stinks," I said, noticing a strong odor of ammonia about it.

I recalled that I'd gotten my camera out before taking Baltho's body to the vet. I'd taken several snapshots of him lying in front of the couch on the green carpet, his mouth open, his tongue falling from the side. The memory was vivid.

Why did I do it? I couldn't imagine ever wanting to see pictures of his looking so awful again.

On the way home, the ammonia smell emanating from the sheet burned my nostrils. The sheet had never smelled of ammonia before. The odor made me weep harder. And choke.

When I opened the townhome door, I noticed how empty the place seemed. Only furniture occupied the echoes. Ghosts stalked the shadows. My house was no longer a home. There was no one there to warm the night. No one to help me face the day. No Baltho. No Figgy–he too had fled.

I walked over to the carpet where my dog had fallen. I could see his energy there. The imprint of his body glowed. I looked at the bottom of the stairs, but I could see no such marking there. I called his name. But no face suddenly appeared. I could feel the tear-floods coming again.

Someone was knocking on the front door. Quietly, but refusing to give up.

In a daze, I answered.

Marilyn stood in the harsh morning light. I must have invited her over. I knew she was diminutive, maybe five-two, but today she looked smaller than I'd ever realized.

Not sure what to do next, nor thinking clearly, I said nothing. I just stood aside and let her in. As soon as Marilyn entered, she noticed the imprint. She pointed it out to me, confirming the same outline that I saw. She knew exactly the position of Baltho's legs, his head, and his body, as he lay in front of the couch, his soul having gone out of him.

Though words came from my mouth too, I was not coherent. I wasn't sure if all the talk was helping or making things worse. I still wanted to rage, to weep—to break things.

"Nothing like having a dog equivalent of the Shroud of Turin right here on my carpet," I remarked, trying to make a joke. I had to lighten the atmosphere. But the remark seemed leaden. It made me burst into another round of heaving and tears.

Marilyn suggested that we drive over to Racine's Restaurant for breakfast. "A change of venue will help you get hold of yourself," she assured me. "You know that only Baltho's body has died. The essence of him still lives."

In the car, Marilyn also noticed the overwhelming smell of ammonia. "What in the world is that smell?" she asked. "Did you clean back there with ammonia?"

I hadn't removed the sheet. I couldn't stand to be reminded. "It's coming from the sheet I wrapped Baltho's body in," I said.

Marilyn reached back to pick up the shroud, which was bunched up on the floor. The smell of ammonia was even stronger. "The smell is making me sick," she said.

"I'm sure the sheet had no such smell before Baltho was wrapped in it," I replied. "I took it, clean, freshly laundered, from the linen closet. I would never have put it away if it had smelled like that."

We were almost at Racine's, so I waited to stop the car and put the sheet in the trunk. There, it wouldn't stink up the inside of the car—at least not so much. I thought about throwing it away, but I couldn't stand the thought of losing a shred of connection with my dog. As I went through the motions, I managed not to burst into tears. "Remembered, if outlived, As Freezing persons, recollect the Snow—" Dickinson's poem continued to stream through my head.

"You need to eat something," Marilyn said. "That's the advice of a Jew. You know how we are. We eat. We eat when we're happy. We eat when we're sad. We eat. So eat," she ordered.

I laughed, but I didn't feel any better. "My mom and my dad didn't have the chance to eat, once they went to the camps. Only afterwards," Marilyn reminded me.

"I know, I know, I've heard your mom's stories more than once." Her dad had died when she was a teenager.

After they brought him to the United States, the Jewish community wanted him to become a rabbi, but he and his wife decided against it. So the community helped him go into business. When Marilyn was thirteen, he was robbed, shot, and made a paraplegic.

"It's a wonder I'm not a blimp," Marilyn said, blowing up her cheeks. "My mom's always pushing food." She was still trying to make me laugh.

It didn't work. "Now I'm thinking of all the suffering in the camps," I said. "Your mom didn't even get a period till four years after she was liberated."

"Yes, and then she got those huge bazooms that she shoves into everybody's face," Marilyn said, holding her hands a foot out from her chest.

This time I cracked a smile.

"We Jews know you have to laugh, even in the midst of tragedy. It's a requirement, a commandment of God."

One of my mother's uncles had been doing family research. He had recently found that an entire branch of the family had been Jews living, working, studying, thriving for centuries in Spain, when Queen Isabella told them that they had to convert to Catholicism or leave. So they left. They went to France, then Holland, then England. By the time they arrived in the U.S., they were Presbyterians. By then, no one had any idea they'd been Jews.

Diasporas everywhere. Suffering and pain, mixed with moments of joy. That is the way of this world.

Five Eyes

For days, I moped, not wanting to do a thing. The oppressive heat continued. I had to hide out in my bedroom with my door closed and the window air conditioner on high all the time or stay downstairs where it remained somewhat livable.

I couldn't do any work at all—no reading, no writing, and no talking with clients. That turned out to be a good thing. I didn't want to disturb anyone with my outbursts, which often turned, without warning, from quiet grieving to wailing.

I recalled what C. S. Lewis said about grief, how often it keeps us from feeling the presence of God, as well as that of the beloved. I knew better than to repress or deny it, for grief is necessary, if we are to pass to a position of acceptance. From there, we can move to faith, hope, and love again.

A few days passed.

One night before bed, I picked a book of modern poetry from my bookshelf. I turned to Dylan Thomas' poem, "When All My Five and Country Senses See." The striking language, the strong rhythms, swept me once more to his ending. Like many writers, Thomas testifies to the endurance of the heart, which will grope awake, even after the five senses have been bludgeoned, for "the heart has witnesses in all love's countries."

In the wee hours of the morning, I was wakened by what felt like Baltho jumping up on the bed. I knew that characteristic jolt as his legs hit the mattress.

I opened my eyes. I saw Baltho's ethereal presence standing there on the bed beside me. With a thump, he lay down as he'd done in the old days, putting his head on my heart.

I wasn't hallucinating. I was wide awake by then. This was no hallucination.

Moments later, the spirit of my neighbor Mona's dead dog Sparkles hopped up, as if the way had been made by Baltho. Good as new herself, Sparkles walked past Baltho. She seemed to want to move up to my face, but, hesitating, she positioned herself in the niche between my head and shoulder. There she curled up.

Sparkles had preceded Baltho in death by months.

Baltho turned his face toward me, looking as happy as he did the day I adopted him. I swore I could feel him, not quite the same as when he wore flesh. Nonetheless, his presence was palpable. So was Sparkles'. Her footsteps, like her body, were much lighter than his, but I could discern them.

Within seconds, the spirits of two other deceased dogs leapt up. They lay on the foot of the bed below Baltho. I was pretty sure that one was the drowned cocker spaniel that had belonged to Adolph's wife when they'd first gotten together.

I wasn't so surprised by Baltho's visit as by his bringing friends with him. If I was just having an hallucination brought on by grief, this component seemed unlikely.

For the next ten nights, I received such visitations. Sometimes, Baltho would bring in dogs that looked like ones from my youth. But as usual, Baltho was the focus, with Sparkles his steady companion.

After the first night, Baltho always let Sparkles jump on the bed first. She'd move to the niche between my head and shoulder. He'd lie a little further down at my side, with his head resting on my heart. As he often did, he'd wrap his forelegs around my arm and put his paw in my hand.

One day I happened to see Mona outside. I asked her where Sparkles liked to sleep. "On the pillow beside my head," she said. "Why?"

I told her about my visitations. At my age, I wasn't terribly concerned if people thought me crazy. I could defend my convictions and thumb my nose if need be.

"Did she try to sleep on the pillow beside you?" Mona asked.

"I think so," I said, figuring that was what she'd desired. "But I don't want any animal sleeping next to my face." I asked when Mona was going to adopt a new dog.

She replied, "I just can't bring myself to do it. I know it's supposed to help. But I can't." She reminded me how Sparkles had gone blind and lost not only her way in the house but her bowel and bladder control. "Often, I'd come home from work and have to scrub my walls and floors before I could get to anything else. I can't face adopting again. There's too much pain." She paused, looking down. "Besides, Sparkles came to me."

I knew how that went. In my dream, Baltho, or the renewed Baltho, found me again. Telepathically, he'd called me to him when he was at the Afghan Rescue five years before. He'd been my own Mr. Dog, the dog who adopted a man.

Once I'd found him, and he'd found me, we faced together the trials hurled our way. Baltho taught me to put bravery on like armor and take up my sword against the forces of darkness, no matter how terrified I felt. He battled illness and affirmed life, brought joy and truth to the kids in the neighborhood and healing to our clients.

Together, we gazed at the sky ablaze with stars and basked in the warmth of day. I watched him dance in the meadows and swim in the ponds, barking gleefully at the geese honking and paddling before him. He reminded me of the splendor of the grass and the beauty of the flower.

Surely Baltho, my Balthazar, my own Mr. Dog, would call me once more. I'd recognize his voice—and go to him—or he'd come to me—restored and whole, the wheel of life having turned again.

About the Author

One of Thomas Ramey Watson's prominent forebears on his mother's side was Jacques LaRamee. A number of places in the upper Rocky Mountain West bear his name to this day. Laramie, Wyoming is best known. Jacques was a renowned and influential explorer and fur-trapper. Because he was just, honest, and treated others well, including the often-despised native Americans, he was held in high esteem. One winter, the story goes, the native Americans were starving, so they killed one of Ramee's cattle. He told his workers not to take action against them—they were hungry. Jacques shared with fellow free-trappers his theory that the world was wide and there was room enough for all. He had the courage to live his convictions and followed the beat of his own heart, not what was imposed on him from outside.

One of Ramee's progeny, psychotherapist, life coach, writer, and professor, Thomas Ramey Watson believes that journeying in various realms—of the mind, the physical world, and the soul—is central to enjoying a good life. The insights gleaned from becoming aware of the intersecting planes of existence lead us to fuller and more deeply lived lives.

Thomas Ramey Watson, Ph.D., is an affiliate faculty member of Regis University's College of Professional Studies in Denver, Colorado. He has served as the Episcopal chaplain (lay) for the Auraria Campus in Denver and taught English for the University of Colorado at Denver. He has trained as a psychotherapist and was named a

Research Fellow at Berkeley Divinity School at Yale University, a position he did not take, choosing to do postdoctoral work at Cambridge University instead.

He is the author of many scholarly writings, including an acclaimed book on Milton, *Perversions, Originals, and Redemptions in* Paradise Lost. His novel, *Reading the Signs: A Paranormal Love Story* will be published soon, as will two books of poetry, *The Necessity of Symbols* and *The Body Is a Map*.

Dr. Watson is available for speaking engagements, teaching assignments, counseling, and coaching. His web address is thomasrameywatson.com. He can be reached at trw@thomasrameywatson.com. You are invited also to join him on Baltho's Facebook page, *Baltho, The Dog Who Owned a Man,* and to order books from the special link on Dr. Watson's website and on Baltho's Facebook page. The book is also available worldwide on Amazon.com and other online sources, as well as in bookstores everywhere. Please request that your local libraries order a copy of *Baltho* too.

A preview of Thomas Ramey Watson's forthcoming novel:

Reading the Signs: A Paranormal Love Story

Synopsis

Ted Jones, university campus chaplain and English Professor in Denver, doesn't need more problems. His life has been full of them. Yet, at the beseeching of the spirit of an old woman, he becomes involved with Sharon, the woman's grown granddaughter. Damaged though she is, Sharon responds. Although Sharon and Ted's trials are multiple, their love forms the crux of the novel. Such love reaches beyond time and space as we normally conceive them, to involve intersecting planes of existence that touch both past and future.

Chapter 1: Vision

The bells of St. Elizabeth's, loud and dissonant, blended for a moment before becoming strident again. They brought back memories of studies in Italy. There, such bells rang out from the landscape and tumbled across the hills into cerulean seas. Here in Denver, the sounds reverberated across campus to snow-covered peaks and reminded me of melodies rising from chaos.

I walked toward the church. The sun shone brightly. A blizzard had blanketed the city the week before, but this morning felt warm. The snow had almost vanished, even in shaded areas. Overnight, the grass had turned from straw to dewy green. Crocuses were bursting into small purple, white, and yellow stars. Like Persephone, spring had returned from Hades, decked in flowery gowns of green. The cycle of life had begun again.

From the sidewalk in front of St. Elizabeth's, I heard a voice. It was coming from the roof. My eyes traveled up the gray granite blocks to a white statue of Mary, a bouquet of roses carved in her hand. I moved my eyes to the stained-glass window behind the statue. The voice came from there.

I stood still and concentrated. I shifted my consciousness slightly to the side. Mystical experiences were not new to me. I'd experienced a number of these phenomena over my thirty-three years. As a professor of English, I specialized in the Great Philosophical and Theological Tradition of the Western World. I'd read the mystics and saints. I was also the Episcopal chaplain for the colleges sharing the Auraria campus.

The apparition of an old woman floating in mid-air appeared near the rose window, a smaller version of those adorning the great cathedrals of Europe. Like a mist moving across the building, her body looked translucent, as fragile as rice paper. Her white hair was pinned at the back, with loose strands falling about the deep wrinkles of her face. Again, she called my name and began to speak in a language that sounded like Russian. She gestured for me to come closer.

Praise for Thomas Ramey Watson's *Baltho, The Dog Who Owned a Man*:

One of my life's quests is to show people that animals are here to teach us compassion and unconditional love. The story of this dog, Balthazar, demonstrates this beautifully. The author weaves a captivating story of the dog that had an innate healing ability as well as being a great teacher. I'm a big fan of this book and convinced it will be loved by anyone who ever looked into the eyes of a dog and saw its soul.

—Jenny Smedley—best-selling author of *Pets Have Souls Too, Pets Are Forever: Amazing True Stories of Angelic Animals, My Angel Diaries, Past Life Angels,* and other books
www.jennysmedley.com

One reason human beings and animal companions forge close bonds is they sense their time together is limited. In *Baltho, The Dog Who Owned a Man*, Thomas Watson doesn't present a story of that bond—he accompanies us on a sojourn of joy, wonder, courage, discovery, compassion, love, healing, frustration, sorrow, and, ultimately, the hope of reuniting some day. Curl up with your pet, along with some tissues, and enjoy a good read.

—Dianne Arcangel—author of *Afterlife Encounters* and *Life After Loss*

Slipping and sliding happily on the fine clothes of a fashionable man, the dog Balthazar, or Baltho, takes the stiffness out of Darren who would present himself always in a full suit of clothes. Head weighing on her lap, Baltho finds Carmen's inner child, as he reveals his own "inner puppy." These are clients of the therapist who owns Baltho, and such fee payers benefit while the therapist wonders.

Thomas Ramey Watson puts up such a cloud of appealing detail for the life of the psychotherapist and his extraordinary Afghan hound that the willing suspension of disbelief is automatic—oh, tell us more about this charming psychic dog, whose first act of esoteric sharing is so strong that the narrative speaker feels his own nose bit by the squirrel that Baltho has chased. The dog has superimposed his own dog vision of the hunt into the consciousness of his owner. But it all hangs together, even for the supervisor of the therapist, Gold, who in some of the funniest scenes I have read in a long time, actually takes the dog to a posh restaurant wearing a "Dog in Training" saddle and orders fancy courses for Baltho, while diners look on.

For those who believe in dogs' powers of the psyche and those who do not, this is a fine book about the inner quest of a dog lover who knows how to narrate the most exotic psychic aspects of the connections between man and beast.

—Alan Naslund—author of *Silk Weather*

Baltho, The Dog Who Owned a Man is a heartfelt story, and so well written it's as if you are there, experiencing every moment. Showing a wonderful personal and working relationship between two beings, the book points out how great animals are and how kind humans can be.
   —Jo Dell Stansel—President, Paws Animal Rescue, Inc. <u>www.pawsrescue.org</u>

www.ingramcontent.com/pod-product-compliance
Lightning Source LLC
LaVergne TN
LVHW041611070426
835507LV00008B/184